California

Wildlife

California Wildlife

Bernard Shanks Number Four

Falcon Press Publishing Co., Inc.

California Geographic Series Staff

Publishers: Michael S. Sample, Bill Schneider
Editors: Marnie Hagmann, Christopher Cauble,
  Rick Newby
Photo editors: Michael S. Sample, Gayle
  Moffat, Steve Morehouse, Chris Cauble
Design and layout: Steve Morehouse
Marketing director: Kelly Simmons

Front cover photo
Mountain lion by Ron Sanford

Back cover photos
Top left: California quail by Jeffrey Rich
Bottom: elephant seals by Frank Balthis
Top right: black-tailed fawn by Thomas
  Kitchin/Valan Photos

Library of Congress Number: 88-83882

ISBN 0-937959-47-2

Design, typesetting, and other prepress work
by Falcon Press, Helena, Montana.
Printed in Hong Kong.

Page 2: *A herd of female desert bighorn sheep cling to the rugged mountains of Southern California. Once eliminated from many areas, they have been transplanted and now thrive on their former range.*
JACK SWENSON

Page 3: *Millions of television viewers were introduced to the sea otter after the* Exxon Valdez *oil spill, when hundreds of the handsome animals were killed. Many people fear that a spill on the California Coast would mean the species' demise.*
JEFF FOOTT

Page 5: *With a wingspan of six to seven feet, the brown pelican glides just above the water along the California Coast. It folds its wings and dives steeply under the surface to feed.*
LEWIS KEMPER

Page 6: *Large ears help identify the black-tailed, or mule, deer. It is the most common large wildlife species in California, in part because of its ability to adapt to change.*
D. CAVAGNARO

Page 7: *The starfish, or sea star, is often seen at low tide along the rocky shores of the state. A quiet carnivore, the starfish feeds on barnacles, mussels, and clams.*
MICHAEL CARDWELL

Acknowledgments

Several friends in the California Department of Fish and Game provided valuable assistance and information that were essential to this book. I appreciate their help and dedication to California's wildlife. Also appreciated are those colleagues and friends in the Center for California Studies at California State University, Sacramento, who encouraged and supported this project. Most critical to this effort was the assistance of Claire Goldstein and Anne Bridges Gavin. Also important to the planning and evolution of this project was Richard Spotts, the California representative of Defenders of Wildlife. He and other conservationists in the state have been vital to the long-term survival of the wild community in California. Most important among these conservationists is Huey Johnson, former secretary of resources, who is both a friend and source of inspiration. Finally, and most important, has been the support and encouragement of my son, Michael Cole Shanks, and my lovely wife, Anne Marie.

About the author

Bernard Shanks was born in El Paso, Illinois, and raised where wildland and wildlife were virtually nonexistant. After graduating from high school, he took a job as a firefighter and fire lookout in Yellowstone National Park, beginning his thirty-year involvement in wildlife conservation.

Shanks attended Montana State University in Bozeman as an undergraduate and went on to complete an M.S. in Earth Science and a Ph.D. in Natural Resource Development.

He has been a park ranger in Grand Teton National Park, Saguaro National Monument, Organ Pipe Cactus National Monument, Grand Canyon National Park, and Petrified Forest National Park. In addition, he worked five seasons as a smokejumper, parachuting to nearly one hundred fires in Alaska and other wilderness areas in the western states. He has taught natural resource management courses at the University of Nevada, Reno, and at Utah State University in Logan.

Active in the political aspects of wildlife conservation in both California and Arizona, Shanks was assistant to the secretary of resources for the state of California and later assistant director for resources, coordinating all federal environmental legislation affecting the state of California. In Arizona Shanks became Governor Bruce Babbitt's major public land advisor. As a result of his work, some sixteen new state parks were approved, a major wildlife refuge established, and other conservation programs developed.

Shanks returned to California as the first director of the Center for California Studies, a public policy institute in the state capitol. Shanks is also the author of *Wilderness Survival* and *This Land Is Your Land*. His articles have appeared in *Sierra*, *High Country News*, *Defenders*, *The Progressive*, *National Parks*, and *The New York Times*. He lives in the Sierra foothills with his wife, Anne Marie, and their son, Michael. The family enjoys camping, hiking, and other outdoor activities.

Dedicated to Anne Marie Ellis Shanks

Contents

California's natural diversity

California has been a "Golden State" for much of its history. It has been blessed with a favorable climate, rich natural resources, and creative and diverse citizens. Wildlife are the living component of California's natural diversity, the resource closest to us in form and function. Wildlife are a source of inspiration, a touchstone for the wilderness from which all life came. They are creatures of incomparable beauty and complexity. As part of our heritage they enrich our lives and bring countless benefits. Each species is worthy of our respect and appreciation.

This book is a testimony to the wildland and wildlife that remain the common heritage of California. If understood, their complexity and diversity will be conserved and protected for the next generation. In all cases, wildlife needs land or habitat. Without it, animals live only in zoos, behind bars and lacking the magical spark of the wild.

Animals require a variety of land, sometimes seasonally, sometimes daily. Habitat is like a home, and the land needed to survive, reproduce, and prosper varies widely. A mouse may need a small habitat, an owl a larger one, and a whale an entire ocean. Wildlife species evolve and change over time. Some have grown into a specific habitat or niche geographically small and precise. The required habitat might be merely fresh water, an old oak tree, or a very specific food or plant. Those animals with flexible diets and habitats, such as the coyote, usually thrive. Those with a very specific food or habitat requirement may find themselves in an ecological dead end. Their struggle to survive continues only with the active assistance and management of *Homo sapiens*.

Other species are threatened by wholesale loss of habitat, like the demise of riparian forests in California. These creatures require land conservation efforts and restoration assistance. As bleak as their survival appears, action is required, not despair. Without habitat, wildlife cannot survive. And in some cases, only humans can now produce the critical land.

California habitats are classified dozens of ways, depending on the inclination of the biologist. Some state agencies and scientists use over two hundred habitat types. This text reduces a complex set of environments to eight easily identified habitat types. Some wild animals are found in all habitats; others are confined to small areas. This book provides an introduction to California wildlife by habitat type with the hope a sense of appreciation will follow.

Change has been the nature of California life. Change first came to California as earthquakes and volcanoes, floods and fires. The earliest hunters came from the north and brought change, even extinction to the region's largest animals. Wildfire, a natural process in the chaparral region, stimulated adaptations in animal life that reduced serious adverse impacts. The earliest pioneers brought livestock and changed the grassland. The water industry, the economic heart of a hydraulic civilization, changed the rivers. Great sprawling cities and suburbs and freeways continue to expand. On any day hundreds of new immigrants arrive from throughout the nation and the world, bringing more human diversity to the state.

Normally, the natural community changes and adapts to stress slowly. In California, these changes have been compressed in time and intensified on some habitats. To all change, natural or man-made, resident wildlife must adapt or die. Human change, such as logging and forest practices, can bring drastic problems, or it can be managed and mitigated to minimize the impacts. Water projects can be designed and operated to reduce impacts on wildlife and in some cases to even improve the present habitat.

Mining can be managed to restore and reclaim land after the minerals are removed. Agriculture can flourish with minimum chemicals and pollution. Entire suburbs can be planned and developed to include parks, wildlife habitat mitigation, and other environmental safeguards.

All of these practices have costs and benefits. Important decisions are now reached through a complex political and economic process which considers, among many other factors, the impacts on wildlife and habitat. California is beginning to craft the policies and procedures to fully protect its wildlife diversity. If it succeeds, California will continue to be a "Golden State," enchanting and magical. ◼

9

Opposite: The slow-moving porcupine, with its shield of 30,000 sharp quills, represents one variety of California wildlife.
TOM AND PAT LEESON

Right: Healthy young brown pelicans offer hope for the next generation. The pelican served as an early warning about the dangers of DDT and other pesticides.
FRANS LANTING

What's in a name?

California gull, California condor, California least tern and rail and mouse and thrasher. The list is long and impressive. California myotis (a bat), California brown pelican, and tree frog and sea lion and vole.

Early California scientists found many new and exciting species, often endemic or "native" only to California, a reflection of the state's uniqueness. As a result, they frequently added *"californicus"* to an animal's scientific name.

Many California species are named after mountains or valleys or regions within the state. There is the Santa Cruz long-toed salamander, and salamanders named after the Tehachapi and Inyo mountains, as well as Kern Canyon and Mount Shasta. Lizards earn their names from the Mojave Desert and Coachella Valley and Panamint Mountains. Cities have character and so do snakes, including one named after San Francisco and another after Alameda across the bay. Santa Barbara named a song sparrow and San Clemente a sage sparrow.

Other California wildlife names provide hints of their worldly travel. There is the Baikal teal, the Eurasian wigeon, Arctic loon, Mongolian plover, Caspian tern, and, of course, the Brazilian free-tailed bat. States throughout the union have their representatives in California, such as the Arizona myotis, Kentucky and Connecticut warblers, and Louisiana waterthrush. Tennessee has a warbler and so does Virginia, and both are residents of California.

Nations are also represented in California wildlife. Few can complain about a nation's identity linked to birds such as the American kestrel, or American bittern, or American wigeon. But what about the American coot? There is the Canada goose, the European rabbit, the English sparrow, and one creature known throughout the world by the name of its homeland, the Norway rat. ■

Wildlife named *California*

California gray whale *(Eschrichtius gibbosus)*

California newt *(Taricha torosa)*

California slender salamander
  (Batrachoseps attenuatus)

California treefrog *(Hyla cadaverina)*

California legless lizard *(Anniella pulchra)*

California mountain kingsnake
  (Lampropeltis zonata)

California brown pelican
  (Pelecanus occidentalis californicus)

California condor *(Gymnogyps californianus)*

California quail *(Callipepla californica)*

California clapper rail
  (Rallus longirostris obsoletus)

California gull *(Larus californicus)*

California least tern *(Sterna antillarum browni)*

California yellow-billed cuckoo
  (Coccyzus americanus occidentalis)

California thrasher *(Toxostoma redivivum)*

California leaf-nosed bat *(Macrotus californicus)*

California myotis *(Myotis californicus)*

California chipmunk *(Tamias obscurus)*

California ground squirrel
  (Spermophilus beecheyi)

California pocket mouse
  (Perognathus californicus)

California kangaroo rat
  (Dipodomys californicus)

California mouse *(Peromyscus californicus)*

California vole *(Microtus californicus)*

California sea lion *(Zalophus californianus)*

California bighorn sheep
  (Ovis canadensis californiana)

Opposite: *The handsome California sister butterfly rests among a field of California poppies.*
D. CAVAGNARO
Above: *The California newt can be seen crawling on the bottom of shallow pools and streams and on land.*
D. CAVAGNARO
Right: *The California kingsnake, known for its shiny skin, is found from Oregon to northern Baja.*
BETTY RANDALL

Mammoths and grizzly bears

Crossed tusks, the huge teeth mineralized in bog iron, mastodons from the drift ice—who knows what happened once when rivers overflowed, when muskeg trapped the last great giants of the Pleistocene?

—Loren Eiseley, *How Brief upon the Wind*

Hundreds of square miles of homes and businesses surround the Rancho La Brea Tar Pit in Los Angeles. The site lies under frequent smog and is passed by thousands of automobiles each day. Yet despite its incongruous location, this large archaeological site provides an important look backward at California wildlife. Within its many excavations, over 85,000 bones and bone fragments have been found from 150 species of birds. Also found were thousands of bones and fragments from hundreds of Pleistocene megafauna, those giant prehistoric animals such as mammoths, saber-toothed tigers, ground sloths, beavers, and camels. All disappeared from California 10,000 years ago.

The rapid disappearance of Pleistocene megafauna is one of the great wildlife mysteries of North America. Late in the last ice age, thirty-two large mammals became extinct, half of them in a narrow time frame 13,000 to 10,000 years ago. Although wetter, the California climate—then as now—was essentially a Mediterranean weather pattern, featuring mild winters and relatively dry summers. Many extinct species were herbivores, which should have found improved conditions as grasslands replaced forests. Furthermore, the animals were mobile and could have migrated in response to food shortages much like African mammals.

At this same time, many plants, amphibians, and reptiles less tolerant of climatic changes escaped extinction. So did almost all the marine mammals. The large megafauna survived an ice age which lasted two million years, yet in a period of a few thousand years the largest and most dominant animals disappeared. What happened?

Some scientists now argue it was the arrival of a "super-predator" which coincided with the end of these impressive creatures. Furthermore, around the world, in Madagascar, New Zealand, and elsewhere, the demise of many major wildlife species followed the arrival of an efficient bipedal predator—man. As today, California in the ice age was a biogeographical island, a refuge for many large mammals seeking mild weather near the coast when glaciers and ice fields crowned the mountains of the West. Wildlife then as now would have been concentrated near water, in valleys, vulnerable, with little chance to adapt to a cooperative predator, a maker of tools, equipped with an oversized brain.

While the merits of this super-predator theory will be debated for generations, man remains the chief suspect as the agent of change in California. These extinctions, recorded in the fossil beds of Rancho La Brea, mark the beginning of a long history of environmental impacts in California.

About 7,500 years ago—several thousand years after the first stone age hunters arrived in California—the first recognizable culture emerged. Living in villages on the coast, these early people relied largely on seafood. Later people became mobile and moved inland where seafood diets were replaced by acorns, seeds, and tubers.

The ability to travel brought commerce and complexity to the native people. When the first European ships arrived, California had the most diverse native culture of any region in America, with six major languages and people divided into more than 50 "nations" and 250 tribes, most with different dialects. The early naturalist C. Hart Merriam estimated that up to 300,000 native Americans lived in California when the first sailing ships approached the western shore. These people represented a wide range of cultural diversity, from the Colorado River desert tribes to foothill acorn gatherers to

Opposite: *Spanish explorers brought horses into the Southwest 400 years ago. By the time of the gold rush, the animal had spread throughout much of California.*
DAVID E. ROWLEY

Right: *After it emerges from its cocoon, the monarch butterfly is a handsome species with great mobility. As a larva, it depends on the milkweed plant for sustenance.*
FRANK S. BALTHIS

coastal boatmen and hunters.

However, one cultural adaptation prominent in the Southwest was not present in California. There is little evidence of irrigated agriculture. Some anthropologists believe the California land was so productive and diverse that irrigation as a human innovation was not essential to survival.

In 1602, the Spanish explorer Sebastian Vizcaino landed near present-day Monterey. The party wrote of watching grizzly bears on the beaches feeding on whale carcasses. The largest and fiercest of the continent's wildlife, the California grizzly bear had no fear of man and frequently attacked, injured, and killed early settlers. But the new pioneers had weapons unlike any the bears had ever encountered, and the California grizzly was menaced by every new settler.

The grizzly originally was found throughout the California Coast and coast ranges, the Central Valley, and into the Sierra Nevada and its foothills. It was absent only from the desert and Great Basin regions. Reflecting the fertile environment, there were more grizzlies in California than anywhere else, and they probably numbered in excess of ten thousand animals.

Unlike bears in colder regions, the California grizzly did not hibernate except in the high mountains. It foraged every month of the year, and settlers frequently encountered the bear. Early historic records include many examples of grizzly bear hunts, attacks, and maulings. The bear was the one wildland creature universally feared. More than any other animal, it was embedded in the myths and legends of Indian and settler alike. Early newspapers sometimes reported five or six people killed and many more injured by bears each year.

The pioneers set out to remove the beast. The animal was shot, trapped, snared, poisoned, and killed with set guns. On the Spanish rancheros the bears were roped and captured for bull and bear fights, a tradition borrowed from the Pyrenees Mountains. These cruel brawls became a common sport at fiestas and public events. With the arrival of the gold rush, miners adopted the fights for weekend entertainment. Towns built arenas for the purpose of hosting such battles. Although the savage activity was criticized, it continued late into the nineteenth century and was banned only after the grizzly was rare. The California struggles between bears and bulls so impressed Horace Greeley he adopted the terminology to describe the stock market on Wall Street, an analogy that persists today.

The last California grizzly was seen in the Sierras in 1924. Sometime during that decade the last bear of its kind died a quiet death deep in the wilderness where it had been driven. Coyotes and magpies recycled the carcass, and the bones, bleached white in the summer sun, were scattered by rodents and porcupines. With the bear's death the California wilderness was gentled, and the darkest shadow became less ominous.

In 1953 the California Legislature named the extinct California grizzly the state animal. Since 1911 the "bear flag" had been the state's official flag, but the 1953 act created the standard design and bear figure used today. The grizzly bear has passed from a living beast to a symbol. Flying over the capitol, in schools, and passing in parades, it is a reminder of the state's wilderness origins.

Yet it was not just the killing of bears which brought change to California. The Spanish brought cattle, sheep, goats, and horses which thrived in the benign environment. Grazed with an intensity never before experienced, many plant species were forced out while many new ones were introduced and spread by domestic stock.

1 5

During the 1849 gold rush, the state was flooded with new arrivals from many countries. "The world rushed in," one observer wrote. Hunters from the gold country depleted the tule elk and other herds of big game within a few years. Market hunting later continued for quail, ducks, geese, and many other species.

Opposite: *California's last grizzly bear was killed in the twenties. The species is nearly extinct in the Pacific states.*
DOUGLAS O'LOONEY

Above: *Few creatures in nature are more endearing than a wild burro and its young. Released into the wild by prospectors, this native of the Middle East has thrived.*
LINDA WEEKS

Several marine mammals attracted hunters from around the world for hides, oil, and fur.

As the technology of the gold rush grew, hydraulic mining became the profitable process to separate gold from gravel. Silt and debris from the large hydraulic operations choked salmon streams, covered salmon spawning beds, and ended salmon runs on many rivers. Then came irrigated agriculture which led to damming the rivers and blocking still more salmon runs.

From the redwood forests on the north coast to the Southern California salmon runs to the rich marshlands of the Central Valley, the demise and displacement of wildlife did not go

16

efforts were misguided, it was a recognition of the importance of wildlife to the state. Today some of these species, such as the ring-necked pheasant, wild turkey, feral pig, and chukar, have become important game species. Others were less successful or less desirable.

Today, the wildlife community continues to be replaced and threatened in California. But throughout the state, wildlife and the laws which protect them are often at the center of successful efforts to stop or control careless development. The sea otter has changed the way billion-dollar, multinational corporations do business. The kit fox alters the projects of land developers and oil companies. The desert tortoise redirects federal land plans on the desert, and the spotted owl reduces logging plans of the U.S. Forest Service. And millions of Californians pass bond issues, join conservation organizations, tax themselves—all to continue the enjoyment of the state's rich wildlife heritage. ■

unopposed. As the population grew and biological sciences flourished, a conservation counterforce emerged. During the crest of the conservation movement at the turn of the century, President Teddy Roosevelt established several large national forests from the public domain. California established the first major state park in 1864, later to become Yosemite National Park. John Muir established the Sierra Club in San Francisco, which became a model of citizen conservation organizations. Other parks followed, including Sequoia and Lassen parks, as well as Death Valley and Joshua Tree national monuments. California developed a park system unrivaled in the nation. Wildlife refuges were created and purchased. A large

and professional Fish and Game Department was established to manage and protect the state's wildlife heritage. Eventually nearly half of California would be conserved in state or federal ownership for its public values, including wildlife.

The demise of wildlife inspired efforts to introduce other species. While some of these

Above: *Extremely destructive to native plants and animals, the wild boar has spread throughout the milder regions of California.*
MICHAEL H. FRANCIS

Opposite: *Federal land managers capture wild horses from the public domain to reduce their numbers and prevent the overuse of rangelands.*
DAVID E. ROWLEY

18

Introduced wildlife changes California

The horse, burro, and pig came to the Golden State as domestic livestock with the first Spanish settlers and escaped to thrive in the favorable climate. Other introduced animals like squirrels and bullfrogs came because California settlers missed the game animals of the East and wanted familiar wildlife in their adopted state. Some turtles and reptiles came via pet shops, bringing pleasure to a child. Then either child or turtle grew, home life changed, and freedom was offered in a mild and benign environment. Even the alligator found its way to California via a pet shop.

Birds like the ptarmigan and turkey came as part of the Fish and Game Department's efforts to expand hunting opportunities. The pheasant from China, the chukar from the Middle East, and the tahr from the Himalayan mountains are but a few wildlife immigrants.

Then there are those hitchhikers who came by accident—the house mouse, starling, house sparrow, and Norway rat—undesirable and unwelcome. They are permanent residents today, displacing native species and impossible

Above: *The South Fork of the Eel River cuts through the Klamath Mountains, offering scenic views and abundant wildlife.*
PAT O'HARA

Opposite: *In a desperate attempt to save the California condor from extinction, all the remaining birds were recently captured. Biologists hope to raise the birds in captivity.*
PERRY CONWAY

to eliminate.

All introduced animals bring change to the state, sometimes beneficial, sometimes not. And all add to California's wildlife diversity.   □

Introduced California wildlife

These wildlife species have been introduced to California:

Amphibians and reptiles—African clawed frog, bullfrog, common snapping turtle, slider (two species), salamander (five species), newt (three species), American alligator, alligator snapping turtle, box and water turtles (twenty-six species), iguanid lizards (eight species), boas and pythons (five species).

Birds—white-tailed ptarmigan, wild turkey, dove (three species), European starling, house sparrow, chukar, ring-necked pheasant

Mammals—European rabbit, gray squirrel, fox squirrel, muskrat, black rat, Norway rat, house mouse, horse, burro, wild pig, fallow deer, sambar, axis deer, Barbary sheep, Himalayan tahr, and feral goat.

Marsupials—Virginia opossum.   ■

The California condor—a bird too ugly to save

Its shadow knew the mammoth and he passed, floated above the sabertooth, now gone, saw the first spearmen on the bison's track, banked sharply, went its way alone.

—Loren Eiseley, *The Condor*

It has been called a "relic of the Pleistocene" because of its steady decline since the last ice age. But more accurately, the California condor, because of its size and the images it crystallized in the mind of men, is a casualty.

At one time this bird with wings as long as small cars was just the largest of the California birds, not the rarest. It once ranged east to Florida, north into Canada, and south into Mexico. Lewis and Clark found it feeding on salmon carrion at the mouth of the Columbia River. A hundred years later its range had shrunk to a few California counties straddling the southern Sierra and coastal ranges.

Its bones are found in some abundance in the Rancho La Brea Tar Pits. Throughout the Southwest its feathers and remains are discovered with human artifacts. Early man and this giant bird met on many occasions. In California Indian mythology, the condor is one of the most persistent images, a part of legend and ceremony.

Biologists are not sure why the condor went into decline. Certainly the stress of development contributed to its demise, and for generations the relationship between man and condor was not healthy, at least for the condor. Before the arrival of modern development, the bird was captured for rite and ritual. With the gold rush came rifles, and the soaring bird with the great wingspan became a more tangible target than an elusive El Dorado. A hundred years ago, egg collecting was fashionable, and the condor's egg—four and one-half inches long, the largest in America—had in the vernacular of today, "market value."

The replacement of elk and antelope with cattle and sheep did not in itself cause problems. The condor did not seem to prefer one carcass over another. But when cattlemen and sheepmen poisoned the carrion, intending to rid the hills of coyotes, the condor's shadow often failed to rise as well. Fast lead and slow poisons were added to the condors' enemies, which had always included golden eagles and black ravens. ∎

Rivers of life

In a wetland, life is richer than in a dense forest, a broad plain, a great desert, or in any other spacious place to which man can retire to recreate his buoyancy of mind.

—Lorus and Margery Milne, *Water and Life*

Freshwater habitats are among the most productive landscapes in California. Along rivers and streams, abundant water supports a unique community of plants and a rich variety of wildlife. Unfortunately, demand for water has reduced the supply, drastically shrinking the riparian community. Even the wildlife which remains must compete with cattle and other domestic livestock for the rich foliage. Riparian lands are largely altered from their original wild state because the same biological productivity so essential for wildlife makes these lands valuable for agriculture.

California had 775,000 acres of riparian woodland in 1850, largely concentrated along rivers in the Central Valley. A ladder of rivers flowed from the Sierra, feeding the Tulare Basin, Stockton, and Sacramento rivers. In the southern Sierra were the Kern, Tule, Kaweah, and Kings rivers. These rungs of the Tulare Basin ladder are now connected with a hydraulic empire of dikes and dams. Farther north up the Sierra Range were the San Joaquin, Merced, Tuolumne, and Stanislaus rivers. The northernmost rivers were the Mokelumne, Consumnes, American, Yuba, and Feather. These streams brought water from the Sierra winter to the Sacramento and San Joaquin valleys every spring.

These rivers and their tributaries formed vast flood basins and large, shallow lakes every spring. Complex riparian forests with abundant and unique wildlife evolved on the natural levees of river silt. The introduction of irrigated agriculture, control of this ladder of rivers by dams, and the diking of river banks all contributed to dramatic changes in the land and wildlife community. Today, the remnants of these productive wild environments are found only in a few wildlife refuges, parks, and conservation areas.

Riparian habitat is often divided into three basic types—river, with flowing fresh water; sloughs or rivers cut off in some manner from the main channel; and marshes which are choked with vegetation. All have abundant freshwater, not saltwater. Each has its own unique community of life. All are highly productive at converting sunlight to biological energy. Diversity is everywhere in the riparian region. So is change.

If you were to ask which riparian creature was the most elegant and the most athletic there might be debate. If you were to add "fun-loving" as a qualification, the only choice would be the river otter. It is probably the most playful animal in the wild.

The naturalist Ernest Thompson Seton wrote, "The joyful, keen and fearless Otter; mild and loving to his own kind, and gentle with his neighbor of the stream; full of play and gladness in his life; full of courage in his stress; ideal in his home, steadfast in death; the noblest little soul that ever went four-footed through the woods."

The otter is an expert swimmer capable of staying under water for many minutes. While

under water the otter closes flaps over its nose and ears, and its pulse automatically slows, helping it conserve oxygen. The otter's webbed feet and strong, streamlined body enable it to outswim fish, its regular food. Otters vary their diets by eating freshwater snails, crayfish, even snakes. It will also eat frogs, muskrats, and, if food is scarce, insects and water plants. The main restriction on its diet is that the food be located in or near water, for the otter's short legs are not built to run down prey on land.

Despite its awkward gait, during the mating season the male otter will hike several miles

Opposite: *A beaver heads for its den with a freshly cut branch. Bark and twigs provide food for the beaver family during the winter months.*
JEFF FOOTT

Right: *Wherever there is water, the Pacific treefrog can be found, from the deserts to the mountains. The suction cups on its feet make it an effective climber.*
JEFFREY RICH

22

Sacramento. Originally found in most of the United States, the otter only needs tolerance and appreciation to thrive. Then its bold and joyous approach to life will assure its survival.

In contrast to the otter, the beaver's demeanor reveals its family tree. It is a rodent, the largest and perhaps most interesting if not exactly dynamic. The beaver is the only wild animal that actually changes its environment to make it more suitable. It cuts trees, dams streams, digs canals, and works diligently. The beaver is the wild kingdom's over-achiever, all work, never pausing to smell the flowers.

Although the beaver is in the same family as the mouse, it is huge, weighing twenty to forty pounds. Some obese individuals, apparently focusing more on eating than working, are said to reach one hundred pounds.

The beaver has a large head with orange-colored incisors driven by powerful jaw muscles. It carves match-book-sized chips out of cottonwood trees, sometimes taking on the largest trees in its quest for dam material. But it is not always a careful worker. The beaver has been found crushed beneath the very tree it cut down.

The beaver is semi-aquatic, needing water to survive. It will build dams as long as a football field and up to eight feet high. On a large river it is content to build a lodge along the bank or to dig a den. The beaver lodge may be fifteen feet across and six or eight feet high, although most are smaller. They are built of mud, limbs, willows, tules, or any other handy material, including debris left by fishermen. The lodge will have an underwater entrance which leads to an inner chamber above water at the center.

Meals for the beaver are the bark and twigs of water-based trees like cottonwood, aspen, and willow. It also favors roots, bulbs, grasses, and tules, and it will store food for winter consumption, especially at higher elevations.

cross-country to another stream. However, it travels not to find water but a mate, signaling its availability by leaving its musk scent on grass and other objects. Females—sometimes several—are attracted to a well-traveled male. Cooperative if not promiscuous, the male may breed with them all during the summer season. It then usually returns to a solitary bachelor life.

The young are born the next spring. Although up to five may be born in a litter, two are most common. As soon as the young can travel, the mother takes them to the water for swimming lessons. Interestingly, they do not appear to be instinctive swimmers. Mother has to coax them into the water for their initial lessons. Once they learn the art of swimming, they play and thrive,

staying with the mother for almost a year until the next generation is ready to be born.

The otter has been trapped and extirpated from much of its original range. However, with management assistance and protection, the brazen otter has pushed into new territory in the Sierra and frolics in the Sacramento and American rivers within the city limits of

Above: *The sight of a great blue heron wading patiently in search of its prey accents any lake or stream. These great birds live for fifteen years or more.*
BARBARA BRUNDEGE

Opposite: *One of fourteen North American species of surface-feeding ducks, mallards lift off in a thick fog from the Sacramento Valley's Butte Sink.*
RON SANFORD

After mating in February, the living chamber inside the lodge may be lined with grass or tender shoots to prepare for the new family. Usually four kits are born each year. The young are born well developed, with their eyes open, and with well-furred bodies up to fifteen inches long. Soon they are active and change their diet from mother's milk to willows and bark. Before long the whole family is busy, storing food and working. The young are evicted only when the next family is due. They must then search out new territory.

The broad scaly tail of the beaver is used as a rudder while swimming, but when diving from some perceived danger, it will flop onto the water with a loud splash, warning others. Another signal system of the beaver is the construction of "sign heaps," piles of mud several inches across. On the piles the beaver deposits castoreum, a scent from large glands on its abdomen. An adjacent gland secrets an oil. Both fluids were used by pioneer fur trappers to lure the curious animals to their traps. Apparently a scent message left on the sign heap caused considerable attention, and any beaver in the neighborhood would rush over to check the latest missive. The oils also gave trappers a unique and memorable fragrance.

The beaver in California and throughout much of the West was trapped almost to extinction in the 19th century. In 1911 the California trapping season was closed and remained closed for thirty-five years. Several thousand beavers were live-trapped and transplanted to the Sierra to expand their range. Once found largely in the valley rivers, the beaver now is located throughout the state wherever there are suitable waters, up to 9,000 feet in elevation.

A smaller relative of the beaver, also aquatic in nature, and with a hairless tail, is the muskrat. It is the size of a cottontail rabbit, with a small head and ears and a tail more like a

24

Norway rat than a beaver. Two musk glands on its lower belly give the muskrat its name. During the mating season, these glands secrete an odor attractive to the opposite sex. At one time before perfume was imported into the United States, women would place their kerchiefs over a freshly caught muskrat to absorb its fragrance, apparently believing it attractive to more than muskrats.

The muskrat has been unpopular with farmers and ditch riders because it burrows into banks and levees, causing leaks. However, for several generations it has been the most popular furbearer and the focus of many trappers.

The muskrat does not create dams like the beaver, but it builds a lodge of tules, mud, and twigs in shallow water or along the banks of a small stream. Although ordinarily nocturnal, the muskrat is easy to see and identify. A vegetarian by nature, feeding on roots, bulbs, and grasses, the muskrat will eat mussels and an occasional crayfish, frog, or other easily captured animal.

Once found only in the northeastern section of the state where it was introduced in the 1920s, the muskrat was transplanted into the Central Valley and spread throughout much of the region. A prolific animal, it raises two or three litters of young a year, sending each generation on its way only a month after its birth.

The most common and best known aquatic animal is the black-masked raccoon. A husky animal reaching ten to fifteen pounds, it has sharp claws, sensitive hands, and a handsome tail complete with black rings.

When evening comes the raccoon emerges from its den, usually near water, and begins to search for food. A female and her young will keep up a chatter or "churring" sound which sometimes is mistaken for a bird. Raccoons are busy and bold. If you are camping nearby they will raid your food, garbage can, and anything

raccoon will dunk its food if possible. Some campers have been amused to see a raccoon, after stealing some bread or crackers from a picnic table, insistently dunk the food into a stream, dissolving most of it except for what was tightly clenched in its fist.

Each spring the female raccoon gives birth to four or five young, which are blind until about their third week. At two months they are weaned and begin short hunting trips, following the anxiously churring mother. She will often take them to shallow water or a lake shore where she will explore under a stream bank or vegetation with her soft and perceptive hands. She may extract a grub, a minnow, or even some young mice. Even these moist foods are habitually dunked before they are eaten. Soon the younger generation follows her example.

These are but a few of the larger and most prominent or interesting members of the riparian wildlife community. The tule elk has been re-introduced into some areas, the ubiquitous coyote is never far, and even the bobcat resides in some sites. In addition to the common raccoon, there is his shy and reclusive relative, the ringtail.

Reptile life is abundant in the riparian corridor, including the western fence lizard, the secretive bulldog-jawed southern alligator lizard, and the western skink, a lizard with teeth.

Other reptiles include the gopher snake, kingsnake, several species of garter snakes, and the racer, a speedy hunter of lizards. In the spring the Pacific treefrog can be heard giving its chorus to signal another season. There can also be found the common native western toad and the huge bullfrog introduced from the eastern United States.

In the spring the riparian wood is flooded with bird song. There are Bewick wrens, rufous-sided towhees, downy woodpeckers, and flickers. Most stunning of the waterbirds,

else of interest. Their search for food has a single-minded intensity, and a foraging raccoon may appear indifferent to you. However, the creature has sharp teeth and claws and, if bothered, a surly temper. Should the family dog decide to pounce on the masked raider, it will think it tangled with a bobcat. The indifferent raccoon will become a biting, clawing, snarling bundle of trouble.

The raccoon is likely the most omnivorous creature in California, rivaled only by the black bear. It will eat birds, eggs, insects, melons, corn, fish, frogs, crayfish, any small mammal it can get its expressive paws on, and anything else it can find.

One odd behavior of the raccoon is to ''wash'' its food whenever it can, a trait that inspired its scientific name, *lotor*, ''one who washes.'' Some have suggested the moisture makes the raccoon's food easier to swallow; others insist the animal just likes the feel of water on its delicate hands. Whatever the reason, the

Opposite: *Rainbow trout are found in the state's cold waters. Steelhead, a rainbow subspecies, migrate into the Pacific and return to their native streams to spawn.*
RON SANFORD

Above: *Today highly popular, the river otter was once regarded as a pest. Almost hunted and trapped into extinction, now it thrives wherever it is protected.*
TOM MANGELSEN

the wood duck makes its nest in the cavities of streamside trees. There is also the barn owl, the tree swallow, titmouse, and the delicate western bluebird. By day there is the diminutive kestrel, the smallest falcon, and at night the little screech owl.

Behind many of the riparian forests, an area of tule marshes averaging ten miles in width once extended 320 miles from Colusa to Bakersfield. Today, most of those marshes are gone but those that remain are among the most important wildlife habitats in California.

One of the most common birds of the tule marshes is the great blue heron, frequently seen watching and waiting for a fish, frog, or even a snake to move within range of its sharp bill. Feeding in the marshes, it prefers to nest in large trees near the river. Other waders include the common egret and the mysterious black-crowned night heron.

Other common birds include the marsh wren, the coot or "mud hen," and three species of blackbirds. Most common is the red-winged and the least likely to be seen is the yellow-headed type. More than likely, any hawk will be the low-flying marsh hawk, also called northern harrier.

Most marsh waterfowl head north in the spring. After spending a mild winter in the valley, some snow geese spend their summers in Siberia, flying in stages from Sacramento to the Soviet Union. Others travel to Alaska and the Yukon and Kuskokwim River deltas, or to Canada—all part of what Aldo Leopold termed "the international commerce of geese."

Several species of ducks summer in the hot marshland, including mallards, cinnamon teals, northern shovelers, American wigeons, gadwalls, and stiff-tailed, proper-looking ruddy ducks.

The rivers and marshes of the Central Valley also hold many species of fish, such as the white

sturgeon, the largest fresh-water fish in North America, and the green sturgeon. Each year several salmon species make their spawning runs up the delta and Sacramento rivers, while bass, catfish, bluegills, and many others comprise the resident river community.

In California, diversity of species and productive habitats are common compared to much of the western United States, and it is difficult to grasp the importance of the riparian and freshwater marsh habitats. Some statistics may help.

California hosts approximately 120 reptile and amphibian species. Riparian habitat supports 83 percent of the amphibians and 40 percent of the reptiles. This environment also

Opposite: *On a California marsh, an American avocet skims the surface for insects. This handsome bird normally nests on bare, open ground or on a mud flat.*
MIKE DANZENBAKER

Above: *Although created by man's mistakes, the Salton Sea now attracts much wildlife, including great blue herons that roost together in large trees along the shore.*
MIKE DANZENBAKER

28

supports 42 percent of the mammal species in California.

While the valley is no longer the important breeding habitat it once was, the wetlands provide wintering habitat for ten to twelve million ducks and geese, hundreds of thousands of shorebirds, and other water-related birds. Throughout the West, the drier the land, the more important the riparian region. The more complex the plant community, the more complex the animal community. Both are highly intricate in California and increasingly scarce.

California's riparian lands were supported by a complicated hydrologic system, now largely simplified and managed for the demands of agriculture and a growing population. As a

Above left: *In Southern California, fresh water may attract the red-spotted toad, normally seen only at night.* TED LEVIN
Above right: *The American bittern makes its home in California marshes.* MIKE DANZENBAKER
Opposite: *During winter, flocks of snow geese are common at Tule Lake and other Central Valley wetlands.* BARBARA BRUNDEGE

result, the riparian wildlife community has been greatly reduced and altered. Today there is a growing appreciation of this wildlife diversity and growing support for its protection. At the same time, water conservation and management is improving along with the ability to restore wetlands. In the future, California will devote increasing conservation energy and resources to the protection and restoration of wetlands. ■

The American River Parkway protects freshwater habitat

One of the best examples of public protection for critical riparian habitat is a green band winding through the capital city of Sacramento and the fast-growing suburbs to the east. The Lower American River Parkway runs for twenty-nine miles below Folsom Reservoir to the confluence of the Sacramento River. Within sight of capital office buildings you can see deer, beaver, coyotes, and even the rare river otter. Bird watchers can find nearly three hundred species along the green and lush river habitat. Under busy streets and freeways, fishermen pull shad, steelhead, and king salmon from clear waters.

Along the river are huge cottonwoods, several types of oak trees, and a complex mix of plant growth providing habitat for a variety of wildlife, including mammals, amphibians, and reptiles. All this is enjoyed by five million people a year in thirty individual "park" areas strung like gems along the greenbelt.

Although a greenbelt had been considered since early in the century, it was not until 1959 that actual land purchasing began. Today, the park connects historic old Sacramento, nearly surrounded by busy freeways, with Folsom Lake State Recreation Area thirty miles up river.

Most impressive about the American River Parkway is its practical usefulness, going far beyond recreation and nature study. The park is bounded along most of its length by dikes which protect the adjoining suburbs from periodic flooding. Yet the dikes do not usually crowd the river. Instead, they are wide enough to permit lush riparian habitat. As a result, the greenbelt serves as a safety net during periodic floods. Most impressive, the park's attractiveness has been a magnet for real estate development. Throughout its length, new housing projects crowd up to the dikes. Properties adjacent to the parkway bring premium prices, proving that conservation can be a good investment.

Back from the brink, tule elk no longer face extinction

The Central Valley grasslands were once the homeland of large herds of tule elk, or "dwarf elk" as they are sometimes called because they average two hundred pounds less than the more common Roosevelt elk. A productive mosaic of grasses in the Central Valley supported herds of elk in the way the Great Plains supported buffalo. Early in the 19th century tule elk were hunted for their meat and hides. Market hunting drove the large animals into the tule marshes where they survived with some abundance until the gold rush of 1849.

By 1854 tule elk were so scarce that hunting was banned throughout the state for half the year, a drastic measure by the standards of the day. But less than a decade later, market hunters claimed to have shot the last cow and her calf in the San Joaquin delta.

Ten years later, the state legislature banned all elk hunting in California. Most hunters believed it did not matter—none of the animals was left. However, the next year San Joaquin Valley rancher Henry Miller discovered elk on his property and ordered them protected. He also offered a $500 reward for information on anyone hunting the animals.

Slowly, skirting the edge of annihilation, the elk on Miller's ranch increased. By 1914 more than four hundred elk were on the ranch, doing thousands of dollars in damage each year. It was time to relocate the animals.

The California Fish and Game Department began transplanting the elk. In 1933 the Owens Valley herd was established. Today it is a source of animals for relocation to Point Reyes, Grizzly Island, San Luis National Wildlife Refuge, and other areas. There are now tule elk in at least eighteen locations in the state, and their numbers are increasing every year. Soon the goal of two thousand tule elk will be reached, an objective established by the California Legislature in 1971 to encourage continued expansion of the herd.

Opposite: *The American River Parkway, which passes through the city of Sacramento, protects wild habitat for mammals, birds, and a variety of fish.*
DANIEL LEE BROWN

Above: *The tule elk was almost extinct by the mid-nineteenth century. Today, tule elk bulls like these healthy specimens ensure the future of the species.*
GARY R. ZAHM

Predators and prey

Looking eastward from the summit of the Pacheco Pass one shining morning, a landscape was displayed that after all my wanderings still appears as the most beautiful I have ever beheld. At my feet lay the Great Central Valley of California, level and flowery, like a lake of pure sunshine, forty or fifty miles wide, five hundred miles long, a rich furred garden of yellow Compositae....

—John Muir

When John Muir first saw California's great valley grassland over a century ago, it was like a living sea, green in April and richly brown in August. Originally twenty-five million acres in size, approximately fourteen million acres of grassland remain today immediately below, and interspersed with, the oak foothills.

The original valley grassland evolved in response to the Mediterranean climate that has prevailed since the retreat of the glaciers. Summers are hot and dry. Winters are mild and wet, bringing six to twenty inches of rainfall. Less than six inches of rain and the valley would be desert. More than twenty inches and the land would be forested.

Unlike the Great Plains, California's grassland had only two grazing ruminants—the pronghorn antelope and the tule elk—and did not evolve with intense grazing pressure from large bison herds. When the first Europeans arrived with cattle, horses, sheep, and goats, the vast inland pasture was grazed more intensely than ever before. Overgrazing and the introduction of over five hundred exotic plant species began a process of rapid change for the grasslands, including a change in the wildlife community.

Once nearly extinct, the tule elk has been reintroduced into several of its native grassland environments. Although most pronghorns are found in the sagebrush grasslands in the northeastern corner of the state, efforts continue to restore the pronghorn into the valleys.

Many of the smaller wildlife species remain abundant. The most conspicuous is the black-tailed jackrabbit, or hare. The hare runs with its long and sensitive ears laid back to protect them from brush, thorns, and damage. Capable of sprinting thirty-five miles per hour, the jackrabbit is a skilled broken-field runner, feinting and dodging to confuse predators.

The jackrabbit needs all its running skills for it is pursued by coyotes, bobcats, horned owls, hawks, and the golden eagle. It is also subject to several parasites and diseases which cycle into jackrabbit populations when they become too high, reducing numbers dramatically.

The true rabbit, or cottontail, is found closer to the woodland, on the edge between the grassland and trees. A major difference between hares and rabbits is their young. Cottontails are born blind, naked, and helpless, unlike the precocious hares. The Nuttall, or mountain, cottontail has up to eight young in each litter and lives near streams and amid the lower hills. Lower in the valley and in the desert areas, the desert cottontail is more likely to be found. Their litters are smaller than the mountain variety, usually having one to five young.

Cottontails and jackrabbits are favorite prey of the wily coyote. Few animals anywhere are more adaptable than the coyote and have survived so tenaciously despite intense hunting, trapping, and poisoning by man. Coyotes are found almost everywhere in California, including the chaparral and brush of Los Angeles, the state's largest city.

Wherever the coyote is found, there are legends, myths, and stories associated with its intelligence and ability to survive. The coyote weighs twenty to fifty pounds, about the same as a medium-sized dog. It spends hours pursuing mice and rodents, but it is an opportunistic hunter. A pair may bring down a sick or injured deer, feast on the eggs of a ground-nesting bird,

Opposite: *A young mountain lion leaps from a rock, intent on surprising its prey. Mountain lions sometimes leap twenty feet or more.*
ROD ALLIN/TOM STACK & ASSOCIATES

Right: *A Belding ground squirrel feeds in the summer sun. At high elevations, it hibernates for up to eight months, the longest of any American mammal.*
D. CAVAGNARO

Of the three fox species, the gray fox is the most common and is found throughout the state, usually below 6,000 feet in elevation. Like the coyote, the gray fox will eat fruit, many rodents, and some birds. When chasing a rabbit or other prey, the gray fox uses its large tail as a rudder to help it turn quickly and react to the feints of the rabbit.

Unlike other members of the dog family, the gray fox will readily climb trees. It will scramble up leaning trees or even vertical ones if branches are near the ground. Sometimes it climbs to escape danger, but at other times it apparently climbs for its own enlightenment. In any case, a fox in a tree always seems a little preposterous.

Like the coyote, the gray fox is usually nocturnal, but not always. However, it is more timid than the coyote and is seldom seen. If threatened it will retreat rather than fight.

Several islands off the California Coast have a small type of the gray fox, which some people call island foxes. Many biologists regard them as a subspecies of the gray.

Red foxes, which actually come in several color phases, are a separate species. Red foxes range across much of the state, generally at higher elevations. A population is now established in the valley, but it may have been introduced.

The smallest fox, the most graceful, and the one threatened with extinction is the kit fox. Sometimes called the "swift fox," it has oversized ears and a slender, almost dainty manner. But it can run with incredible bursts of speed, catching some of the fastest prey. Of the three major fox species in California, the kit is most associated with the valley region. It prefers the arid, open, sandy ground favored by kangaroo rats and mice. Several foxes may den in the same proximity, giving the impression they are sociable. Kit foxes often feed on kangaroo rats and rabbits but will take birds, gophers, and many kinds of insects, including Jerusalem crickets, grasshoppers, ants, scorpions, and spiders.

A subspecies of this animal, the San Joaquin kit fox has been declared rare under the Endangered Species Act. This fox hunts at night and spends its days in a den. Its home range is relatively small, but it may use four or five shelters during the year. The pups are born in large brood dens. Unpaired foxes will use a smaller den until they find a companion.

Coyotes sometimes prey upon kit foxes, but more often they fall victim to poachers or automobiles. When they are learning to hunt, the young are vulnerable to starvation. Their

Above left: *Spring brings hot, dry days that evaporate vernal pools and give rise to a carpet of wildflowers. Later in the year, the pools may dry up completely.*
TUPPER ANSEL BLAKE

Above right: *During the winter months, the vernal pools fill with rainwater and soon attract thousands of insects, water birds, and other aquatic life.*
TUPPER ANSEL BLAKE

or tip over a suburban garbage can to find something edible. The coyote will stuff itself with fruits, nibble on green grass, or snack on grasshoppers with equal relish. Unlike many predators, it will eat frogs, snakes, and certainly any small bird or mammal it can catch. When hungry it will worry a porcupine and try to seize its soft underbelly, or venture to the edge of a highway and feed on roadkills.

Given the coyote's flexible feeding habits, it is not surprising some coyotes develop a taste for domestic lamb, if available. However, research shows that coyotes do not eliminate a band of sheep but assess a tax of 5 to 7 percent on the unprotected lambs.

People with pet cats or small dogs sometimes become upset over the coyote's choice of food. The mild house cat or carefully manicured poodle that wanders from its yard one night may encounter the bright eyes of a coyote. The dog may be a cousin to the coyote, but years of interbreeding and domestication have made

Opposite: *The Diablo Range is typical of the rolling hills and oak forests that lie above California's hot Central Valley.*
TUPPER ANSEL BLAKE

Above: *Young red foxes venture outside their den. Shy and nocturnal, the fox eats fruits and vegetables as well as insects, mice, and other small prey.*
RICH KIRCHNER

it an easy meal for the lean and clever coyote. The same is true with house cats. Breeding and refinement do not impress the coyote. It is first a survivor and always a predator.

Coyotes mate late in the winter, and the young are born in about two months. Usually the parents find an old den but will settle for a hollow log, cave, or an old badger den. If necessary, they will dig a long tunnel in good soil. Three to nine pups are born, weak and wobbly. The male hunts for mother and pups during the first few weeks. When the pups first venture out, they may fall prey to bobcats, owls, and other predators. Once they are grown, coyotes have few enemies except for man.

As coyote pups mature, they join the adults on hunting trips. There they adopt the hunting habits modeled by their parents. At this time some people see a family and form the mistaken impression that coyotes hunt in packs. At first the apprentice hunters are inefficient. By winter when their skills are developed, young coyotes are forced to find their own territory.

The high-pitched yipping, barking, and yodeling of the coyote is a magical sound of nature. In many campgrounds and on the edge of most California cities and towns, coyote music can be heard many nights each year. To the uninitiated the many cries seem to come from several voices, but usually it is but one coyote practicing his call for reasons best known to himself. It remains a wild sound and a tribute to an animal unintimidated by modern man and his works. Sometimes he even seems to be laughing.

In addition to the coyote, the valley grassland contains several of the state's predators, including the badger, gray fox, and kit fox. To many, a fox appears like a diminutive form of coyote. However, the three fox species in California are all more sensitive and vulnerable than the coyote.

hunger often drives them to roads and highways where they feed on roadkills. One consequence is a high mortality of young kit foxes that fail to learn about automobiles and bright danger speeding out of the night.

For the kit fox, coyote, and other predators, small mammals provide basic nutrition on the grasslands. One of the mainstays is the California ground squirrel, which might be mistaken for the gray squirrel except that it seeks shelter in burrows rather than trees. Ground squirrels lead a colonial lifestyle, sharing a network of tunnels and dens. Snakes, rabbits, toads, skunks, and burrowing owls often join the extended family of a ground squirrel colony.

California ground squirrels are opportunistic eaters, feeding on green spring vegetation and shifting to seeds and nuts in the summer and fall. They also eat meat, feeding on both young quail and eggs. Along roadsides they will dine on flattened animal corpses and will even cannibalize their own kind.

When summer temperatures are high in the

Above: *A young kit fox displays elfin curiosity while staying close to its burrow. The kit is the smallest of the American foxes and the most threatened by extinction.*

TUPPER ANSEL BLAKE

valley grasslands, ground squirrels spend the hot period in their burrows in a biological stupor termed estivation, the seasonal opposite of hibernation.

Once regarded as a valley and foothill animal, the California ground squirrel has spread into the mountains as high as 10,000 feet. Logging, grazing, and road construction have opened areas in the forests, and the ground squirrel has moved aggressively into these new habitats. Today, this squirrel is probably seen more often than any other native wildlife.

It is not surprising the ground squirrel is so numerous. After breeding in the spring, adults give birth in about a month, three to fifteen young to a litter, with an average size of seven. In two months the young are on their own.

Because of their fertility and their habit of feeding on agricultural crops, ground squirrels are widely disliked. In some areas they burrow into canal banks, causing leaks in levees and irrigation ditches. In other areas, fleas associated with the squirrel sometimes carry bubonic plague, and the squirrels are poisoned. Many regard ground squirrels as the major wildlife pest in the state and have encouraged the protection of predators to keep them under control.

Smaller grassland residents include the Heerman's kangaroo rat, which like the pocket gopher has fur-lined cheek pouches that serve as small shopping bags. It stores seeds and vegetable matter for stormy winter days, and, like all others in this family, it does not drink but survives on "metabolic water" produced within its body from carbohydrates. It also takes frequent dust baths to rid itself of insect pests and to keep its coat in good condition.

Another mainstay of the valley grassland community is the western harvest mouse, which may be mistaken for the common house

37

mouse. The harvest mouse feeds on a wide variety of seeds, green vegetation, and fruit. It even eats small insects.

The mouse reaches maturity at four months and will give birth to litters two or three times a year, each with an average of four or five young. The young are born deaf and blind, but within two weeks they are weaned from mouse milk. Usually two weeks later, they are out of the nest foraging for food. Once out in the world, they are fodder for many predators, including hawks, owls, and foxes.

Another common resident of the Central Valley grassland is the San Joaquin pocket mouse, which, like the pocket gopher and kangaroo rat, has deep fur-lined pockets on both sides of its mouth. A nocturnal creature, it

spends its nights foraging for seeds, stuffs them into its pockets, and carries them to an underground den for more permanent storage. Retiring from the night's activity early in the morning, it prudently plugs up the entrance to its burrow with dirt. Like other fast-living small mammals, it will have several litters a year, each with several young.

The ornate shrew is the only shrew common

Above: *The black-tailed jackrabbit uses its large ears to listen for its many predators and to cool its body in the heat.* JEFF FOOTT

Opposite: *Highly territorial, a mountain lion checks the scent on a stump. Although adult lions can travel far, they generally confine themselves to one region.* PAT AND TOM LEESON

to the grassland but is one of twelve species in the state. Like others in its family, the ornate shrew is mouse-sized, beady-eyed, with a long pointed nose. Shrews feed largely on insects and spend most of their lives looking for food. They are literally a nervous bundle of energy. Besides the usual roster of predators, a shrew's enemies include trout and mergansers, who dine on water-oriented shrews.

Feathered representatives of the grassland include the killdeer, mourning dove, horned lark, and especially the meadowlark, whose song seems synonymous with a spring day in the grassland.

The cooler-blooded animals include the ubiquitous western toad and western spadefoot. The speedy western whiptail and racer are two common lizards in the valleys, along with archaic-looking coast horned lizards.

Few temporary works of nature compare to the pools found every spring in the California valleys. Once referred to as "hog wallows," California's vernal, or springtime, pools are becoming more appreciated as they are more understood.

Each winter with the first rains, these small depressions with a hard-pan floor begin to fill with water. When spring comes, a unique array of plants begins to bloom.

Some two hundred plant species are restricted to vernal pools, including an entire plant tribe. While vernal pools are most often appreciated for their unique plant life, at least five kinds of fairy shrimp are endemic to them. The California tiger salamander, a declining species, relies on the pools for breeding habitat. Other invertebrates of the pool environment are known to exist but have neither been described nor understood by biologists.

The vernal pool environment is complex, and more than seven types of pools have been identified. They vary in size from puddles to those several acres in area. More important, the climate, soil, and geology combine to create such numbers and diversity of vernal pools only in California. More than any other environment in the state, vernal pools are unique.

When the rains end each spring, the pools begin to dry. In the process, more and more surface is exposed, and concentric rings of green give way to outer rings of flowers. Finally, the dry, brown, outside rings close in on the pool, the blooming flowers, and greenness. The sun and dryness snuff out the vernal pool for another season. But while they last, they are like drops of rich living color, ponds of beauty and life. And like all of nature, their cycle reminds us of life's beauty, delicacy, and transience. ■

California's controversial cat

Probably no other animal in California has been more controversial than the mountain lion (*Felis concolor*). The recent proposal to reopen a hunting season on California mountain lions after a fifteen-year moratorium unleashed old fears and conflicts. This concerns an animal few people will ever see in the wild, an animal so solitary and reclusive that finding and watching it without the help of dogs or radio collars is the experience of a lifetime.

Once common throughout the United States, mountain lions were reduced by hunting and predator control programs. One by one, states finally ended their bounty and control programs on the big cat. California ended its bounty system in 1963 after 12,500 mountain lions were killed over a 56-year period. Less than ten years later, concern over their very survival resulted in closure of all mountain lion hunting.

Mountain lions live up to fifteen or more years in the wild. They weigh from eighty pounds for a small female to two hundred pounds for a large male. Their habit of preying primarily upon deer has earned them the hostility of many deer hunters. The thought of a mountain lion killing a deer nearly every week, all year round, infuriates some hunters who demand control of their efficient competitors. Biologists believe mountain lions play an important ecological role by weeding out the sick, old, and otherwise unhealthy deer, keeping the rest in relative health and abundance. Without mountain lions, an entire population of deer might be stricken with disease and wiped out.

Despite many stories and legends, experienced mountain lion hunters insist the big cat is not aggressive or dangerous. They are shy, easily treed by dogs, and almost passive when cornered. Nevertheless, the mountain lion is feared, and recent attacks on people, while extremely rare, have created support to open up mountain lion hunting in California once again. Fuel was added to this movement when a child was attacked by a mountain lion in Southern California in 1986.

Sportsmen and the California Fish and Game Department are pushing for a limited season on mountain lions. At the same time, several conservation groups have vowed to oppose the hunts with lawsuits and political pressure. Controversy will surround the tawny animal for years to come. ■

Life in the suburbs

These small creatures would cling to us, to things human if we would let them. They would keep our land sweet and wholesome for them and for us.
—James Norman Hall

Once on a Marin hilltop in the Golden Gate National Recreation Area, I watched a bobcat intently stalk mice in a green meadow. From where I sat, the San Francisco skyline, Golden Gate Bridge, and weekend sailboats on the bay were all visible. Hundreds of automobiles flashed in the sun on a freeway. For many minutes the bobcat made me oblivious to the technology and urban life in the distance. Its intensity was mesmerizing, until a quick dash and shrill squeal broke the spell.

The contrast between California's wild community and its urban life is most striking in the chaparral environment. About 80 percent of the state's population resides in a coastal belt forty miles wide from Santa Rosa to San Diego, and most of this area is chaparral. Overall, chaparral covers more than 8.5 million acres in California, and it forms one of the state's two hilly habitats. The oak-covered hills surrounding the Central Valley form the other.

Both plants and animals, including man, have had to adapt to periodic wildfire in the chaparral environment. By consuming tons of fuel per acre, fires stimulate new green growth that helps sustain wildlife populations. Ironically, once the chaparral burns, it is virtually fireproof for several years and acts as a firebreak.

After years of trying to stop the annual cycle of fires, the California Department of Forestry adopted a chaparral management plan that includes prescribed, or controlled, burning. The result is a mosaic of fresh growth that safeguards residential areas, reduces firefighting costs, and supports increased numbers and types of wildlife.

The largest native herbivore of the chaparral is the black-tailed deer, once considered a distinct species because of its dark color. Today, biologists list it as a subspecies of the mule deer, the West's best-known large mammal. After the chaparral burns, nutritious green growth sprouts with the first rains, and deer populations prosper for about seven years. As the brush matures, the quality of the forage—and deer populations—decline, awaiting another fire.

Mule deer are found throughout California from deserts to mountains, foothills to dense forests. The coastal animals tend to be smaller and darker. The Sierra version is sometimes called the "granite phase," and those from the northeastern corner, termed "lava" bucks, are larger and favored by sportsmen.

Deer are dependent on brush or browse, unlike elk, which graze primarily on grass.

Because of this, they thrive after fires in the chaparral, after clear-cutting in the pine forests, and after other changes that bring brush where mature trees or thick grass once flourished.

Other than man, deer have few enemies. The most impressive is the mountain lion, which can kill up to fifty deer a year. In the past, sportsmen tried to eliminate mountain lions under the mistaken impression they were protecting deer. Instead, lions may keep deer populations healthy by taking diseased or weak animals. Coyotes seldom hunt deer, although they will take fawns and injured animals. A more serious threat are packs of dogs near suburbs that run deer down and kill them.

More fawns would fall victim to dogs and coyotes except for their natural advantages. First, fawns are born in the spring, when fresh green plants provide extra shelter. The young deer have spots for the first sixty to ninety days that help them blend into the surrounding terrain. Most important, fawns instinctively freeze when a threat is near. They lie down, stretch out on the ground, and do not move, even if you walk right by them. Unhappily for predators, fawns have virtually no odor

---

Opposite: *Normally active at night, a sleepy-eyed gray fox ventures out into the sun. The gray is the only member of the fox family that regularly climbs trees.*
LAURA RILEY

Right: *Sulphur butterflies color a field like an Impressionist painting. Unfortunately, this butterfly's larvae are the targets of agricultural chemicals.*
D. CAVAGNARO

42

and cannot be detected by even the most sensitive nose.

The brush rabbit, a smaller relative of the cottontail, is another denizen of the chaparral. A shy creature, it rarely ventures far from the cover of the brush and elfin forest. By producing three or four litters in a season with three to six young in each one, this rabbit uses its reproductive capacity to outlive predators. And the predators in the chaparral country are several, including the bobcat, gray fox, reclusive ringtail cat, and coyote.

The bobcat is a common predator in the brush country as well as throughout the state. Found from the floor of Death Valley to the tundra and alpine areas above the timberline, this adaptable animal also can be found on the urban fringe like the coyote. Ranging east to Florida and Maine and throughout much of the United States, the bobcat preys on many species, including rabbits, ground squirrels, mice, pocket gophers, and wood rats. But it is not reluctant to prey on quail and other birds. If the opportunity presents itself it will take lambs, poultry, and piglets.

Bobcats usually weigh fifteen to twenty-five pounds, but a heavyweight may go to thirty or more pounds. Their young are typically born in the spring, blind and dependent on the female for several months. When it is time for nature's cycle to begin again, the male courts the female, yowling like the largest alley cat in the country. The blood-curdling screams may go on for several hours until the female accepts the suitor. Apparently, the vocal display of desire has little to do with affection. Once the mating is complete, the male is not heard from again—at least for another year.

In the wild the bobcat has few enemies. If approached, it gives an impressive performance of hissing, growling, and spitting. Like a domestic cat, it can stiffen its fur and pretend to be twice its true size. Most predators, no matter their size or their appetite, do not regard the hostile bundle of fury worth a meal.

Reptiles are numerous in the chaparral, including the western fence lizard, southern alligator lizard, and the western skink. Most dramatic is the coast horned lizard, which feeds on ants and other insects while it wanders around looking like a miniature Triassic reptile, armored with spikes and horns.

One of the most common snakes in this environment is the gopher snake, the state's largest. Mice make up the bulk of its diet, but it has the ability to capture and eat squirrels and rabbits as well.

The speediest snake is the striped racer, holding its head high like royalty. If threatened, it quickly climbs up into and onto the thick canopy of chaparral and races off. Lizards are its preferred prey. More than any other snake, its range is restricted to the chaparral.

The oak woodlands surrounding the Central Valley are the state's other hilly habitat. Many of the oaks in this nine million acre area are

Above: *A graceful coyote, springing into action, falls on a vole. Warm spring days often find coyotes in meadows hunting with child-like intensity for these bite-sized morsels.*
EUGENE FISHER

Opposite: *Livestock grazing, tree cutting, and urban sprawl have diminished the oak woodlands of California, critical habitat for many wildlife species.*
TUPPER ANSEL BLAKE

44

unique to California. Fifteen of the sixty-eight species of oak in the United States are native to California, and nine of these are found only here. Some one hundred species of birds depend on the oak trees in California for the large variety of insects they provide. Acorns are found in the diets of thirty-seven mammals. In turn, many other creatures are tied to those that depend directly on the oak forest, creating a second tier of life contingent on the oak tree.

Oaks are a favorite habitat of cavity-nesting birds like woodpeckers, flickers, wrens, nuthatches, swallows, western bluebirds, kestrels, screech owls, and others. Barn owls and wood ducks nest in large oak cavities whenever they can. The trees also serve as platforms for crows, hawks, and great blue herons.

Under the canopy of the oaks, America's heaviest land bird makes its home. The wild turkey was abundant in the East and the symbol of Thanksgiving for three hundred years. Although not native to California, the turkey's reputation as a game bird led to efforts

to introduce it as early as 1908. The initial attempts used birds imported from the Southwest, a mix of wild and domestic stock. Repeatedly, these birds failed to survive anywhere in the state.

Meanwhile, the turkey population nationally continued a hundred-year decline. By 1930 the total turkey population in twenty-one states

Above left: *The badger, a powerful digger, is often scarred from fights. It usually feeds on ground squirrels, but sometimes eats rattlesnakes.*
RICH KIRCHNER

Above right: *Winter snows force mule deer out of the high mountains. On the lower slopes, the animals find the nutrition essential for survival.*
MICHAEL S. SAMPLE

was only 20,000. Biologists began studying the big bird, and many attempts were made to start new flocks. As recently as ten years ago, a study found 354 attempts at introducing 350,000 game-farm turkeys in twenty-one states ended with 331 total failures.

Managers gradually improved their ability to trap and transplant wild stock. They discovered that game-farm birds, even with 95 percent wild genetic stock, were unable to make the transition to wildland. Slowly, through research and good management, the turkey has been established in every state except Alaska. Since its low point of the 1930s, the turkey population has increased 10,000 percent nationally to an estimated two million wild turkeys.

In the California oak woodlands, the turkey is found in at least twenty-four counties. Birders and hunters find a bird that may weigh up to twenty-five pounds. Mating begins as early as February with expressive strutting displays by the male. The female finds a remote spot and lays from five to seventeen eggs on the ground. Soon after hatching, the young begin foraging with the mother for insects and green leaves. Within two or three weeks they can take short flights.

Turkeys are extremely wary and difficult to find. Usually their large impressive tracks are seen on trails before any bird is sighted. The view most people have is of a bird with enormous drumsticks sprinting off into the woods at an astonishing speed. Although they can and do fly, turkeys run like track stars. Throughout the year, they are an interesting addition to the wildlife of the foothills.

Another reclusive animal of the foothills is the dark-eyed and shy ringtail. Because of its nocturnal habits, it is the most elusive of its family. Only a little larger than a gray squirrel, the ringtail has short, smooth fur and a tail nearly as long as its body, complete with seven black-and-white bands.

Gold rush pioneers often kept ringtails around their cabins as mousers. Their sharp claws, agility, and nighttime habits earned them the name "miners cat." While they subsist mainly on mice and rodents, they also eat fruit, berries, and occasionally acorns.

The foothill environment is regarded as the ringtail's home range, but these animals are also found in riparian forest communities in the Central Valley and on brushy slopes from Oregon to Mexico. They range from sea level to 6,000 feet in the Sierra Nevada. Although they are almost always found near water, there are ringtails in the desert canyons of Southern

California.

Spotted and striped skunks are two other reclusive predators of the oak woodland habitat. Neither animal is a good runner or fighter, relying instead on chemical warfare. With a foul-smelling scent gland located at the base of its tail, the skunk can spray an oily scent ten to

Above: *The shy ringtail is better at hunting mice than a cat. In winter, it wraps its lush tail around its body for warmth.*
CHARLES G. SUMMERS, JR.

twenty-five feet. When the animal stamps its feet like a child having a temper tantrum, this is skunk body language meaning "back off." Sometimes the spotted skunk does a handstand on its front feet, arching its rear end over its head in your direction. It may also spread the white fur of its tail over its body like an umbrella. Such gymnastics may look cute, but in reality, the skunk is improving the aim of its spray.

The largest of the two species is the striped skunk, which grows to about the size of a plump house cat. The spotted variety is about half that size and lean like a weasel. Both are omnivorous, eating fruits, eggs, insects, rodents, reptiles, and even carrion. Both are nocturnal

and commonly smelled rather than seen.

The striped skunk lives in the hills near farmlands but, as many people sense, sometimes ventures into suburban neighborhoods to forage for food. It favors brushy areas near water while the spotted skunk is more tolerant of dry and rocky hillsides. Although both are found throughout much of California, the spotted skunk is the less common.

Another animal found not only in the foothills but throughout much of the state is the badger. Related to the skunk but larger and more powerful, badgers have been seen from the floor of Death Valley to the ridge tops of the White Mountains above 13,000 feet. It is most common from the Central Valley floor up to 5,000 or 6,000 feet elevation.

The badger has the short, squatty appearance and behavior of a veteran brawler. With a flat, broad head and long claws, it deserves its reputation as a tenacious fighter. Its strength and explosive reaction to any threat protects it from almost every predator except man and mountain lion.

During California's pioneer days, the dubious sport of "badger baiting" was practiced at county fairs, rodeos, and other public events. A sleepy-looking badger was placed on a wood pile or in a barrel, and bets were taken that no dog could beat the badger. It was rare for the badger to lose, leaving many dogs bleeding and hurt from the encounter. Appropriately, this "sport" was banned early in the century.

Unlike the fleet fox or coyote, the badger does not rely on speed to capture its prey. It takes a much more direct approach. It simply digs its prey—gophers, ground squirrels, and other rodents—out of the ground. When the powerful badger has finished its methodical, almost leisurely digging, a meadow will look plowed, with mounds of dirt and burrows everywhere. And the local population of rodents will have been reduced.

So efficient is the badger that a hiker may see one digging in a meadow and then flattening out to hide. As the hiker approaches, a flurry of activity erupts as the badger furiously digs itself out of sight.

A badger's underground den is easily recognized by its size, ten to twelve inches across, and by its oval shape, tailored to fit the badger's profile. The young are born in the spring and within weeks are practicing their digging to find mice and rodents. With their keen noses, they tenaciously excavate rodents from the soil like furry little potatoes.

One of the favorite foods of the badger is the pocket gopher, of which four to fourteen different species are found in California, depending on who is classifying the animals. The most widespread is the valley pocket gopher, found throughout much of the state. Its many variations in color and size contribute to the confusion as to how many species there really are.

The pocket gopher's most notable characteristic, besides the mounds of dirt it digs up, are its external cheek pouches. Fur-lined and reversible, these pouches are used to carry food or nest material. They have large, yellowish-colored incisors that are usually exposed in a toothy grin. An accomplished digger, the animal burrows under the soil looking for roots or tubers. When it finds a choice plant, it eats the root, leaving the stem and leafy parts above ground to dry up and die. More than one gardener has been shocked to see a favorite plant like a petunia disappear into the earth with a series of sharp jerks. The pocket gopher, having found an especially tasty meal, has pulled the entire plant into its burrow.

Gophers must carry their dirt out to the surface to clean the passageways of their burrows. With patience you can watch one emerge at the mouth of a tunnel, holding an armful of soil against its chin, and forcefully throw it several inches onto the mound. Predators such as hawks, owls, herons, foxes, bobcats, coyotes, and the family cat also patiently watch these fresh mounds to pounce on the gopher. Since weasels and gopher snakes can pursue the gopher into its burrow, it often plugs the hole with dirt when it has completed its digging.

Gophers do not hibernate in winter but, in the mountains, work under the snow, feeding on the stems of plants and making stashes of food. They continue to dig and bring their dirt into snow tunnels. When spring comes and the snow melts, long snakelike earthen cores, forty feet or longer, lie on the surface of the ground. Like castings of some exotic creature, they are evidence of the pocket gopher's winter labors. In farming areas, gophers open holes in irrigation ditches and create problems for farmers. They have their beneficial purposes as well, like almost all wildlife, adding one more dimension to the diversity of life in California. ∎

Above: *For this mule deer, death in the Tuolumne Meadows in Yosemite National Park does not mark the end. Nature depends on the recycling of energy and nutrients.*
MICHAEL FRYE

Opposite: *Rooting in wet soil, a feral pig can dig up large areas of bulbs and roots in its voracious search for food. It also eats rabbits, birds, snakes, and amphibians.*
MICHAEL H. FRANCIS

Feral pigs

They come down from the chaparral hills and forested canyons at night to root in Marin County gardens, some of California's most expensive real estate. Early morning runners encounter them on the trails of several state parks. The feral pig *(Sus scrofa)* is common throughout much of California. "Man has always known the hog," it has been said. Today front page news stories, television reports, and cartoons demonstrate this truism.

Although domesticated by the Chinese 6,000 years ago, the porker has been the object of hunters since the dawn of civilization. The first pigs in California were brought by the Spanish in the 1700s as domestic livestock. In the 1920s, the European wild pig was introduced to Monterey County for sport hunting. Today a mix of both varieties ranges over much of the state where summer temperatures are not extremely hot and winter temperatures seldom fall below freezing. This description covers a substantial area of the state—two-thirds of all the counties—including the coastal ranges, valleys, and foothills.

Today, the pig population is estimated at 70,000 to 80,000, and over 30,000 are harvested by hunters each year. How does the feral pig continue to prosper under such hunting pressure? First, a young pig becomes sexually mature at six months. As many as a dozen piglets are born into each litter, and the average usually exceeds six. Two litters are born most years unless there is a drought or other stress on the female. Finally, a mature pig has few enemies except man and the mountain lion. Combine the birth rate with a notoriously indiscriminate appetite, and the prospect for a multitude of pigs is high.

It is the hog's indiscriminate palate that has raised the concern of many conservationists. The pig prefers oak mast (acorns fallen on the forest floor), but also roots up a wide range of plants and vegetable matter. It can be a serious predator. The young of ground-nesting birds such as quail and small mammals like rabbits are easily located by the exceptional nose of the feral pig and gobbled up.

The pig does not have sweat glands and must find water and mud to cool itself in hot weather. These springs and water sources are key habitats for many amphibians as well as delicate plants. The hog does not mind—it will feed on snakes, reptiles, amphibians, or anything else that comes along.

Park managers and those concerned with maintaining wildlands often go to expensive lengths to keep pigs under control and from dominating their environment. If its wide range of acceptable foods and impressive reproductive energy were not troublesome enough, the lowly pig is regarded by those who have studied it as a highly intelligent animal. While its eyesight is poor, its hearing and sense of smell are exceptional. Hunters find the feral pig one of the most popular and challenging game animals in the state. ■

All creatures great and small

Come to the woods, for here is rest...

—John Muir

On the north coast lies a slender band of relic forest. Once spread over much of the northern hemisphere, these woods are the home of the redwoods, the world's tallest trees, growing to a height of 370 feet. The redwood forest covers only 2.3 million acres in the fog belt, a sinuous ribbon averaging ten miles wide and penetrating only 42 miles inland at its widest point. With the year's rainfall sometimes totalling 100 inches, supplemented by 40 inches of fog drip, the redwood forest is the southern extension of the rain forest that stretches to Alaska.

The largest and most localized of the animals of this area is the Roosevelt elk. A subspecies of the more widely dispersed Canadian elk, this animal is darker in color and adapted to the Pacific rain forest. The bulls' fall bugling, their annual challenge to competitors, is one of the most thrilling sounds of the wild. The fierce fights between bulls, with antlers clashing, over harems of cows are unforgettable.

Today, there are few predators to prey on the Roosevelt elk, except mountain lions and coyotes, which limit their ambition to only young or disabled animals. Instead, elk numbers are restricted by competition with domestic livestock and other agriculture activities. Once threatened with extinction, the elk is now thriving in most of its territory.

One of the most unusual animals found in the dense rain forest is the mountain beaver, a primitive mammal species. Called a "boomer" by some people in the region (although its voice is a whimpering cry), it doesn't resemble a beaver either in appearance or habits. The mountain beaver is about a foot long with a short, stubby tail and resembles a large, overgrown pocket gopher.

The closest most people get to this odd nocturnal animal are the many holes and burrows it excavates. Often located near streams and in dense ferns or other thick cover, even the entrances are commonly hidden by plants and brush. The mountain beaver feeds on a wide variety of plants and stores piles of food in haystacks. While it does not cut down trees, it strips off needles and bark for food.

Other inhabitants of the rain forest include the raccoon, ringtail, and porcupine. Predators include the bobcat, gray fox, and coyote. Also widespread in the coastal forest is the efficient and handsome mink. Unlike the closely related marten and fisher, the mink spends much of its time in and around water. As large as a house cat but leaner, it has the most attractive fur coat of any animal. An excellent swimmer capable of catching robust fish, the mink also feeds on frogs, crayfish, mice, rabbits, muskrats, and birds, including water birds.

More than one birdwatcher has pleasantly watched a duck on a pond, only to have it turn into a thrashing, quacking casualty as a mink erupted beneath it like a shark. After a kill, the mink sometimes stores ducks or other prey, especially its favorite, the muskrat, in a burrow. Like the skunk, the mink has a foul-smelling scent. If attacked, it puts up such a fierce battle, hissing and spitting, that few predators are willing to confront the animal. Only the silent great horned owl occasionally drops out of the night sky and slips its sharp talons into the mink's brain, bringing death before its rage explodes.

The dark forest hides the smallest of the meat-eaters, the hungry shrew. Three species of this mouse-sized predator—the Trowbridge, vagrant, and Pacific shrews—are found on the forest floor. Shrews prey largely on insects but will eat slugs, snails, and other invertebrates. With the highest metabolic rates of any mammal, they must consume their body weight every three hours. They hunt day and night and live such a hectic life that old age comes within sixteen months.

Opposite: *The bobcat appears harmless and curious, but in reality, it is a capable predator with a wide choice of habitats. Its mottled coat serves as effective camouflage.*

D. CAVAGNARO

Right: *The western gray squirrel is the only gray tree squirrel on the West Coast. Active on all but the stormiest days, the western gray feeds on nuts, berries, and insects.*

TOM AND PAT LEESON

The shrew has been the topic of much research because of its small size and runaway metabolic rate. It is now believed that as warm-blooded animals get smaller, they must increase their metabolic rate to maintain a constant body temperature. The masked shrew, weighing only four ounces, is likely the smallest mammal mother nature could ever design.

At first glance the shrew might resemble a mouse, but it travels with such speed, making such quick and jerky movements, that its behavior can belong only to one animal. There is nothing timid about the shrew; it seems oblivious to danger. While it probes and searches for food, it persists with a high-pitched twittering sound. Males, in particular, often have intense fights that leave them scarred and sometimes crippled.

In the summer, females give birth to young the size of honeybees, sometimes up to ten in a litter. Usually they are weaned within a month, and the female has a second and occasionally even a third litter the same summer. Some of the young survive by their

Above: *The mountain beaver resembles a woodchuck more than it does its namesake. This rodent has the odd habit of sharpening its teeth on baseball-sized rocks.*
TOM AND PAT LEESON

Opposite: *Black bears range in color from blond to cinnamon to brown, but this black lives up to its name. Black bears have a wide-ranging diet that includes dandelions.*
TOM AND PAT LEESON

quickness, but most nourish a variety of predators, transferring their intense energy another step up the food chain.

The initial impression of some observers is that the redwood forest lacks birds and wildlife. More careful inspection reveals several interesting species. The pygmy nuthatch, red crossbill, hermit warbler, and solitary vireo are found in the canopy. On the ground, rufous-sided towhees, dark-eyed juncos, and white-crowned sparrows nest and forage. They are quiet, furtive, and unobtrusive in the peaceful forest.

The great exception is the raucous pileated woodpecker, eighteen inches long and with a wingspan over two feet. It is distinguished not only by its size, which makes the bird one of the largest woodpeckers, but also by its cap or crest. Its flashing color and strident cries make it easy to identify. Little wonder that locals often call it the "cock of the woods."

This big woodpecker prefers to live in mature fir, aspen, and redwood forests where rotting trees provide an abundance of ants, beetles, grubs, and other insects. Its long bill can rip apart bark and rotten logs efficiently, if not cleanly. It uses its tongue, which can extend four or five inches from the tip of its bill, to probe for insects, deftly fishing them out.

The mild but moist climate of the coastal forest creates ideal conditions for amphibians. Most numerous are the salamanders, the largest of which is the Pacific giant salamander. Also found in the area are lungless salamanders, including the attractive blotched ensatina, which draws all its oxygen through its smooth, moist skin. The far-flung western toad, found throughout most of California, is the only toad inhabiting redwood country.

Reptiles include the western fence lizard, the western skink, and the northern alligator lizard. The only venomous reptile is the widespread western diamondback rattlesnake. Some reptiles are very specialized, such as the sharp-tailed snake, which feeds entirely on slugs. When it is dry and slugs are rare, this snake retreats underground to await conditions more favorable to slugs rather than change its diet.

A forest much different from the coastal rainforest forms a wide band on the western slope of the Sierra Nevada. The dominant tree, the ponderosa pine, circles the northern end of the Central Valley and grows in the higher mountains of the coastal ranges above the fog and redwood belt. Biologists further subdivide California's forests into other subgroups, each more detailed and complicated than the last, but the conifer, or montane, forest is a useful division to begin to identify several interesting wildlife species.

The largest animal of the forest, and the one most consistently identified with it, is the black bear. Although its long, dense fur is commonly black, it comes in many colors, including cinnamon brown, yellowish brown, and even tinged with blue. Adult bears weigh 200 to 300 pounds, but they can be quite obese. The California record is 680 pounds. While the black bear may appear clumsy because of its shuffling walk, it climbs trees readily, runs if necessary, and can be as quick as a cat. Black bears, as many people know from experience, are usually nocturnal, raiding camps, picnic tables, and garbage cans as campers sleep. Although bears may be bold in parks like Yosemite, they are usually shy and seldom seen, except as they crash off through the brush when surprised on a hiking trail.

The black bear is omnivorous, eating plant or animal foods, whatever is convenient. It often feeds on carrion but rarely preys on domestic livestock or large wildlife species like deer. In the spring they graze on fresh green vegetation much like a cow. They are fond of berries, insects, fruits, fish, and honey. In some

5 1

of the quills lie flat and are nearly concealed by the porcupine's thick, dark fur. The quills are attached to a muscle layer beneath the skin, however, and when threatened, the animal can raise its quills, providing an effective defense. If attacked, the porcupine sweeps its tail—and sometimes its entire body—around, driving dozens of needle-sharp quills into the flesh of its attacker.

Pliers are usually required to remove these quills from the family dog. Although some quills may be scattered by the sweeping action of the tail, the porky does not "shoot" its quills like darts. It may lose several hundred quills in a close encounter with a dog or predator, but they are soon replaced by a new crop.

Other than man, the only animals to prey on the porcupine with much success are the mountain lion, wolverine, and the aggressive fisher.

Most of the time porcupines feed on the cambium layer, the underbark, of pine trees. They also consume pine needles, and during colder months, mistletoe. Like many rodents, they gnaw on bones and the shed antlers of deer, apparently for the minerals and calcium they contain.

Their young are usually born in April or May of each year, and there is typically only one to a litter. Because of the long gestation period, the baby porcupine is born large and well developed, nearly a foot long and weighing about a pound. Its eyes are open, teeth formed, and its body covered with dense black fur

concealing hundreds of quills about an inch long. As soon as the fur dries, the quills become hard and sharp. On its first day, the baby instinctively displays its quills and swings its tail quickly if startled. In two days the young one is climbing trees, and within ten days it is weaned but stays with its mother for up to six months.

Initially the porcupine seems dull and clumsy. Surprisingly, they like to play and will frisk around with pine cones or small sticks like a puppy. The mother and young porcupine will wrestle with lots of grumbling and whining. Those who have adopted young animals insist they are a gentle and interesting pet that displays intelligence and affection.

Squirrels are part of the native wildlife in almost any forest, and California's is no exception. Because tree squirrels spend most of their time in trees, they have adapted differently than their ground squirrel cousins. One difference is the lack of cheek pouches in tree squirrels. They leisurely feed in the relatively safe tree environment and have little need to store food quickly or transport it efficiently to the safety of a burrow.

California has three native species of tree squirrels, the largest of which is the gray squirrel. A handsome creature with a full bushy tail, it is comfortable not only in mountain pines but also in foothill oaks and in Central Valley trees in cities such as Chico and Sacramento. In urban areas the gray species is sometimes confused with the eastern fox squirrel, which has been introduced to the state.

Like most squirrels, the gray loves to feed on nuts and acorns but also eats mushrooms. It builds a nest of leaves and twigs but prefers to claim a woodpecker cavity to rear its young each spring. While the gray squirrel seems agile and often jumps from tree to tree, it cannot keep up with its more energetic cousin, the Douglas

areas, acorns are a mainstay of their diet.

Bears normally avoid people. But every year bears injure campers, often in the process of getting to camp food or when people attempt to feed them. Unprovoked attacks are extremely rare, and by keeping a clean camp, hanging food out of reach of bears, any contact you have with them will likely be interesting and rewarding.

Next to the bear, the animal most often associated with the forest is the porcupine. Much smaller, slow, and shuffling, with short ears and button eyes, the "porky" looks like easy prey. Its defense, of course, is its unique coat of thousands of sharp, barbed quills. Many

Above: *The Pacific giant salamander is a formidable-looking creature that frequents damp forests and cold streams. Unlike most of its kind, it can be found during the day.*
LARRY ULRICH

Opposite: *These twin mule deer fawns will soon lose their spots. After her first pregnancy, a healthy young doe is likely to give birth to twins.*
BILL HEAD

Despite its name, this squirrel does not ''fly.'' Instead it has a membrane extending from wrist to ankle on either side of its body that forms a gliding surface. It leaps from near the top of one tree and glides down to the lower branches or trunk of another.

Unlike the other two native squirrels, the flying species is less particular about what it eats, feeding on birds' eggs and insects of all kinds and stages of development, as well as nuts and acorns. Around an unprotected camp, it readily eats crackers, prunes, meat, cheese, and other picnic supplies.

The flying squirrel is much more common in California than many people believe because of its reclusive and nocturnal habits. The young are born in the spring, hairless and with their eyes closed, usually in an old woodpecker cavity. When born, the gliding membrane is transparent. If threatened at this stage, the mother takes the young in her mouth and sails off to a safer location. The young are weaned in approximately five weeks and make their first solo flights in about two months.

squirrel or chickaree.

The climbing and jumping ability of the chickaree is impressive, and it so prefers trees that it seldom spends time on the ground except to drink and gather nuts. While in the trees it is curious, noisy, and most of all, active. The chickaree will climb 200 feet to the top of a sugar pine or even the giant sequoia, go out on the thinnest branch, and cut loose a cone. After it has cut several loose, the chickaree descends to the ground, gathers the cones near the trunk, and begins to open them and extract the seeds. If it is not hungry, it stores the cones in the moist ground.

If the chickaree is the most agile of the squirrels, the flying squirrel is the smallest and most difficult to see. Active at night, the animal comes to most people's attention by the steady rain of twigs and cones it drops on a forest camp while the occupants are trying to sleep. Either late in the evening or early in the morning, the camper may be startled to have a flying squirrel suddenly plop against a tree trunk like a furry pancake.

Above left: *Anna's hummingbird is one of the only hummingbirds to spend the entire year in California.*
BETTY RANDALL
Above right: *The face of the porcupine looks harmless. However,* *thousands of quills cover its back and tail.*
JEFF FOOTT
Opposite: *A Roosevelt elk bull ventures into a meadow from his dark north coast forest home.*
TOM AND PAT LEESON

Other wildlife of the forest include several species of bats, the largest of which is the hoary bat, two to five times as large as any other species in the vicinity.

Reptiles in the forested region are diverse but seldom seen by the casual visitor. The most striking and beautiful is the rare California mountain kingsnake, marked by contrasting bands of black, white, and red. It preys on the only venomous reptile of the forest, the adaptable western rattlesnake.

The most common member of the lizard family is the western fence lizard, found throughout the nondesert areas of the state and often called locally the "blue-bellied swift." One of the more unusual lizards is the northern alligator lizard. The female increases the survivability of her eggs by retaining them in her body until they hatch.

Amphibians include several frog, toad, and salamander species. One of the most common is the Pacific treefrog, another is the foothill yellow-legged frog, which ranges well into the pine forest. Several types of ensatina occur in the forest lands, but more common is the California newt, whose functional lungs permit it to forage under dryer conditions.

While the ponderosa and other large conifers are important to wildlife, it is the California black oak, dispersed with the ponderosa pine, that is most critical to deer and black bear as well as many other birds and mammals. Deer have been known to consume up to 85 percent of all the acorns that fall, preferring them to all other foods. Bears eat an average of 315 acorns during each fall day they are available. Both deer and bear gain important fat from the oak mast during the fall, essential for winter survival.

A tale of two owls

Owls and logging in the Northern California national forests seem unrelated to most people. But the two subjects have stirred controversy and have been a headache for land managers. In part, the personalities of two owls underlie the issue.

The center of concern is an appealing bird with large, dark, soft eyes, *Strix occidentalis,* the spotted owl.

Long a favorite of birdwatchers, the spotted owl is gentle and trusting. It seldom flies when found during the day, and a female sitting on eggs can be lifted off the nest without protest. The other owl is the large great horned owl, *(Bubo virginianus).* Fiercely antagonistic, the great horned has earned its nickname, "winged tiger."

The peaceful spotted owl, when approached, follows a person by turning its head almost full circle, then flipping its head around so quickly only a blur can be seen. It has endearing facial expressions and the habit of winking one eye then the other while watching birdwatchers.

In contrast, the great horned owl has been known to come out of the night and attack campers without provocation. The bird is noted for bold, slashing attacks often coming soundlessly. Scores of documented cases record severe injuries to the head, throat, chest, and back of birders who have approached the nest of the great horned owl.

The spotted owl, also known as a "hoot owl" because of its distinctive call, loves to groom itself and preen its feathers. After landing, it shakes its feathers and carefully preens each one with the tip of its beak. So carefully does it groom itself that the owl sometimes falls asleep in the middle of the process.

The great horned owl regularly attacks and eats skunks. Few are captured that do not reek of skunk aroma.

The easy-going spotted owl usually feeds on mice or small rodents. But campers may find it carefully picking over their picnic table, perhaps sampling a bit of melon or cleaning up discarded fish heads.

The great horned owl eats and preys on almost anything. It can swallow an entire Norway rat in one gulp.

The spotted owl has extraordinary hearing, having the ability to locate a mouse running across rock 150 feet away. So sensitive are the owls' ears that during unusually long rainy periods in the north coast forests, young owls starve to death. The constant dripping of the rain from the trees interferes with their ability to locate prey, acting like static on a radio.

A pair of spotted owls may seem to many birdwatchers close, helpful, and almost tender toward each other. A pair of great horned owls caged together, even if well fed, do not live in peace. Eventually the female kills and devours her mate.

Why is there a controversy over logging and these two owls? The spotted owl must have the dense cover of a mature forest to survive. If the forests are clear-cut into open blocks, the peaceful spotted owl is hunted down and killed by the great horned owl, exterminated from the scene. Survival for the spotted owl requires an old-growth forest. And for birdwatchers, its survival is a personal concern. The great horned owl seems quite capable of taking care of itself and doesn't need logging to help it survive. ■

Above: *The great horned owl's large, yellow eyes are one of the distinguishing characteristics of this extraordinary predator.*
TED LEVIN

Opposite: *The spotted owl is today the center of a political controversy over the amount of old growth forest necessary for the owl's survival.*
TOM AND PAT LEESON

Life in the high country

And from the eastern boundary of this vast golden flowerbed rose the mighty Sierra, miles in height, and so gloriously colored and so radiant, it seemed not clothed with light, but wholly composed of it, like the wall of some celestial city. Along the top and extending a good way down, was a rich pearl-gray belt of snow; below it a belt of blue and dark purple, marking the extension of the forests; and stretching along the base of the range a broad belt of rose-purple; all these colors, from the blue sky to the yellow valley smoothly blending as they do in a rainbow, making a wall of light ineffably fine.

—John Muir, *The Yosemite*

Above the dense forests lie the mountain meadows, subalpine areas, and still higher alpine regions—the highest, coldest, and windiest land in California. The smallest of the state's major environments, alpine lands cover less than 1 percent of California. They are the most remote and least altered landscapes, consisting almost entirely of public land managed by the Forest Service and National Park Service for wilderness recreation and national parks.

In the mountains as elsewhere, biological boundaries are dynamic, responding to variables such as temperature, rainfall, sunlight, and elevation. Timberline is at 11,400 feet on Mt. San Gorgonio in Southern California, but drops to 10,700 feet on Mt. Whitney and 8,800 feet in the Cascade mountains near the Oregon border.

Elevation brings changes in vegetation. On high and windy ridges near timberline, the whitebark, limber, and lodgepole pines are twisted into nature's bonsai trees. Plants at this elevation also are found in northern Canada and Alaska, and a true arctic environment exists near the glaciers on Mt. Shasta.

Many wildlife species also respond to elevation changes. While animals such as the mule deer, coyote, and red-tailed hawk are adaptable and may be found from sea coast to valley to timberline, other animals are more site specific.

The snowshoe hare is a permanent resident of the alpine region, surviving under extreme winter conditions. Alpine California is one of the most southern areas of the snowshoe range. It is found north to the Arctic Circle throughout much of Alaska and Canada. The snowshoe hare has adapted to the high mountain meadows by developing large hind feet which provide support on the snow, and by twice-a-year molts. Most snowshoes have brown or mottled fur during the summer months, but during the winter the pelage becomes snow-white, aiding in escaping the attention of predators. Like other species of rabbits and hares, the snowshoe populations fluctuate greatly, sometimes in eleven-year cycles.

Elevation causes adaptation and segregation of wildlife. The gray squirrel buries surplus seeds and acorns in underground caches during the fall. During the winter when food is scarce, the squirrel returns to these food caches. However, above six thousand feet the snow is deep nearly every winter, forcing squirrels to find food that is buried under several feet of snow.

The chickaree squirrel successfully lives at higher elevations with a change in habits. It stores nuts and seeds in piles near its home. A scientist once found over 1,200 sequoia cones in one pile. Since piles are large and easy to find under snow, they provide a survival advantage compared to the gray squirrel's scattered plantings.

The food storage behavior of the gray squirrel is not the only characteristic that confines it to lower elevations. Compared to the nervous chickaree, the gray squirrel is slower and less agile. At higher elevations the pine marten is more common, and the marten is easily the squirrels' most feared nightmare.

Martens climb and jump as well as squirrels, and once a marten begins a pursuit, a squirrel's

5 9

Opposite: *Fast water, damp rocks, and the plump body of a water ouzel are common sights along mountain streams. The ouzel sings its monotonous song all year long.*
LARRY ULRICH

Right: *The golden chest patch and bright eyes mark this animal as a pine marten. Sometimes hikers can coax a marten from its den by imitating a mouse's squeaks.*
GERRY REYNOLDS

life expectancy is short. To see a marten chasing a squirrel is to witness panic and desperation. The squirrel may leap from the highest tree and fall to the ground in its frantic effort to elude the determined marten. In this race for life, the chickaree is Olympic class compared to the relaxed gray squirrel. Along with deep snow, the pine marten keeps the gray squirrel from the chickaree's territory.

During the winter the pine marten hunts dense forests above six thousand feet. During the summer it ranges higher to open areas near rock slides and meadows. With its great speed and agility, it is a quick and efficient predator. A golden brown chest patch and lush fur coat make it one of the most beautiful mountain hunters. For generations its fur has been prized by trappers from the edge of the Bering Sea to the east coast of Newfoundland and Nova Scotia, and from the Arctic Circle to the southern Rockies and Sierra.

The handsome marten is curious and may investigate a mountain cabin or picnic table. Hyperactive, it has a grace unique to the family, but also a short temper and solitary habits. Its family characteristics include a set of musk glands which release a noxious fluid. Unlike some mountain dwellers, it does not hibernate but grows winter hair on the soles of its feet for protection from the snow and cold.

The marten has few enemies, but one exception is its close cousin the fisher, which is faster and stronger. Rare in California, the fisher is fox-sized, weighs about ten pounds, and is usually found at lower elevations than the marten. Although named ''fisher,'' this predator feeds on small mammals such as squirrels, wood rats, mice, marmots, and birds such as quail and grouse. Most interesting, the fisher is one of the few predators to consistently hunt and kill porcupines, and they are seldom found without quills in their hides. Apparently their

hunting technique is simple. They flip the sluggish porcupine over and attack its vulnerable underside, ignoring sharp quills earned in the process.

Several predators commonly seen at lower elevations are seldom encounterd above timberline. These include the gray fox, badger, mountain lion, bobcat, and snakes. The coyote, long-tailed weasel, red-tailed hawk, and great horned owl do range to timberline and alpine areas.

California's smallest predator is the ermine, or short-tailed weasel. The male weighs six ounces or less, the female just half as much. The short-tailed weasel has a high metabolic rate and is a fearless bundle of nervous energy. What it lacks in size it makes up in skill, agility, and raw aggressiveness. The ermine prefers small rodents to any other type of food and will kill and consume over one thousand mice and other rodents in a year. Each day it eats the equivalent of one-third to one-half of its body weight, usually as red meat.

Like the snowshoe hare, the ermine changes from a drab brown color in the summer to a white coat in the winter, except at lower elevations where it may retain part or all of its brown color. It is distinguished during the winter by its black-tipped tail. Occasionally a great horned owl or pine marten will prey on the ermine, but the weasel is so courageous that few predators try to make it a meal. The weasel itself shows little hesitation in taking on prey twice its size, dispatching the victim with a bite through the skull.

Adaptable as well as courageous, the weasel is often seen around cabins and tents occupied

Opposite: *Mount Dana, rising just over 13,000 feet, is one of many spectacular Sierra Nevada peaks.* MICHAEL S. SAMPLE
Above left: *Transplanting has helped reintroduce* *bighorn sheep into California's mountain ranges, where they once thrived.* PATRICK CONE
Above right: *The wolverine is a rare sight in the high Sierra.* RICHARD P. SMITH/TOM STACK & ASSOCIATES

by humans. Cross-country skiers in the Sierra are sometimes surprised by the black-eyed beast popping up out of the snow to see if they are a prospective meal. After a quick check the animal will bound off, blending into the snow except for its black-tipped tail.

A slightly larger relative of the ermine, the long-tailed weasel is also found in the Sierra and throughout much of the state except the low deserts. Like the ermine, it will change color to white in snow country, and their ranges often overlap in the mountains.

The largest member of the weasel family and the rarest animal in the California mountains is the legendary wolverine. Normally associated with the far north country in Canada and Alaska, a few individuals reside in the high Sierra and Rocky mountains. Few people ever see a wolverine in the wild. Most of what is known about it has been passed down by trappers, including its reputation as a "glutton" or "skunk-bear."

While the animal is nothing like the "demon of the north woods" as portrayed in popular fiction, it is a solitary animal, living in the most inaccessible regions of California. When seen it is usually at or above timberline.

The wolverine may be three feet long and can weigh up to forty-five pounds, resembling a small bear. It has long claws and a powerful body like the badger. Like all weasels, it has a scent gland under its tail, and, although it doesn't spray the scent like a skunk, it does anoint its leftover prey to discourage dining by other animals.

During the summer the wolverine will prey on marmots, rodents, and porcupines. In the winter, it does not hibernate but continues its restless search for food. It has been known to

prey on snowbound deer several times its own weight. The range of the wolverine is circumpolar, but is rare throughout much of its range, in part because the female rears only two or three cubs every two or three years.

Tracks of the wolverine resemble the coyote or mountain lion. If you find a fifth toe mark, you are witnessing the fleeting marks of California's rarest animal and should consider yourself most fortunate.

Cold-blooded reptiles and amphibians are intolerant of low temperatures and therefore few species can be found in the high country. One of the most unusual exceptions is the Pacific treefrog, which is found to 13,000 feet. A gaudy little frog, only an inch or two long, it is strikingly colored with greens, reds, or

browns. A black eyestripe is constant, but it can change its body color in a few minutes.

An amphibian unique to one small section of the Sierra is the Yosemite toad. Generally found from 9,000 to 11,000 feet, the highest of any of the seventeen American toads, it hibernates from October to June. Each summer in the mountain meadows near Tioga Pass, it can be seen walking across snowbanks on its toes. After mating the eggs are laid in shallow ponds where they are solar heated and develop quickly. Within seven or eight weeks they are transformed into toadlets, move to land, and have but a few weeks to feed and grow before they hibernate.

The toads are preyed upon by California gulls and Clark's nutcrackers, but most predators avoid them because of their chemical defense. Like most toads, when attacked they ooze a noxious, sticky secretion that is unappetizing to many predators.

Another unique alpine species of the Sierra is the golden trout, native only to this environment and designated the state fish. Named for its bright colors, including lemon-gold and orange, the alpine fish was originally found only in the upper reaches of the Kern River. First carried from its home water in a coffee pot during the summer of 1876, it is now found in many Sierra lakes and streams. While the fish does survive below 6,300 feet, it thrives at elevations from 8,500 feet to 10,500 feet. In streams the fish is only five to eight inches long but grows from twelve to eighteen inches in mountain lakes. More than any other fish, the golden trout is a treasured species identified with wild and rugged high country.

At the upper reaches of the alpine country, bird life is rare. Only two native bird species nest in the windswept alpine rock fields. One is the horned lark, which nests on the ground in a spot usually partially sheltered by a rock or other windbreak. Perhaps because of the wind, the lark has developed a walk instead of a hop like most birds. The other is the water pipit, which also nests on the ground and walks instead of hops.

A number of birds venture into the alpine regions to feed on seeds and insects. One of the most common is the rosy finch; the most striking is the mountain bluebird. The white-tailed ptarmigan was introduced into the Sierra in 1971 and now nests in selected areas.

There are approximately thirty other bird species found in the subalpine and alpine regions of the mountains during the summer. Only ten remain during the winter. Most migrate or move downslope in the fall to more moderate environments. One exception is the blue grouse. It spends its summers in the lower forests but travels uphill in the fall to the treeline among red firs, which provide the bird's sole winter food.

The most common winter bird in the Sierras is the small but noisy chickadee. These active birds form bands and feed on dormant insects in conifer trees. One of the birds' favorite foods is the larvae of the lodgepole pine needle-miner. The mountain chickadee opens the needle with its bill and skillfully extracts the tiny caterpillar.

John Muir's favorite Sierra bird was the plump water ouzel, "a singularly joyous and lovable little fellow." As Muir pointed out, any waterfall or rapids would have the ouzel bobbing up and down, ready to plunge into the fast and cold water in search of aquatic insects. While in their submarine mode, the bird has a scaly trap door over each nostril to keep out water. It also lowers a filmy membrane over its eyes, like a diver's mask, to keep the water from interfering with its vision.

If the water is not too fast, the ouzel merely walks upstream, poking in the gravel for insects. If the current is strong, it will spread

its wings underwater and fly to a calmer spot. Even on the coldest winter day the ouzel can be seen plunging into fast water looking for bugs. To rest by a Sierra stream on a summer day and see the little ouzel walking on the bottom of a crystal-clear stream, the sun reflecting off the air bubbles around its body,

Opposite: *During its winter phase, the long-tailed weasel is entirely white. Its supple body seems to flow through the snow like a dancer's, but it is a fearless predator.*
TOM AND PAT LEESON

Above: *Alert ears and watchful eyes are often the first thing a hiker sees of a black-tailed, or "mule," deer—just before it bounds away for cover.*
PAT O'HARA

is a magical experience.

Several high country mammals hibernate during the long winters. The fat marmot seen by many summer hikers does not venture out during the winter. Also called a rockchuck, it is the largest member of the squirrel family, but it neither climbs trees nor resembles its agile cousins. It prefers to feed on meadow forbs, sunbathe on granite rocks, and grow fat for the long winter. When marmots come out of hibernation in the spring, they set out to find a mate. As is often the case in the mountains, the young are born only a few weeks later. Within two months they are mature enough to be on their own.

Chipmunks, ground squirrels, and jumping

64

will face each other, and at some almost unseen signal, charge and butt their powerful heads and horns together. After several teeth-jarring encounters, the strongest may win out or the two may just tire and start feeding, ignoring the females. Unlike elk, smaller males are not excluded from breeding after the struggles. Some biologists have described the fights as largely ritualistic.

Bands of sheep in the Sierra are so skilled at traveling across rugged terrain and avoiding people that they are seldom closely encountered. However, on occasion alpine hikers and climbers will approach bighorns from above, blocking their normal escape route to higher ground. Under these circumstances the sheep may let you get closer and closer, all the time growing more nervous, until they bound around you and climb at a fast run to gain their natural position above you.

Sheep are found only in a few isolated areas of the Sierra, but recent management efforts using trapping and transplanting have expanded their range and assured their restoration to many of their native mountain ranges. ■

mice share much of the same habitat as the marmot and follow the same life cycle. Serious eating and fattening during the summer is followed by a long hibernation, when metabolic rates fall and fat is slowly burned off.

Few wilderness sights are more striking than the bighorn sheep in its rocky and rugged setting. Bighorns are regal summer dwellers of the eastern Sierra high country, although in the winter they are found on lower slopes.

A fully grown ram may weigh 250 pounds, but females weigh only half as much. Unlike deer and elk, the bighorns do not shed their horns each year. Instead, after the first two or three years of rapid growth, a decreasing amount of horn is added each year. The horns, which bear distinctive growth rings, complete a full circle or "curl" after thirteen or fourteen years.

In the fall, horns are the rams' major weapons as they fight for ceremony if not the right to sire the next generation of lambs. The largest rams

Above: *Lady beetles, or "bugs," here seen hibernating, are well-known and respected predators of aphids and scale insects, making them welcome in any California garden.*
FRANK S. BALTHIS

Opposite: *The pika, shaped like a guinea pig, is a common sight in the high Sierra. During summer, pikas keep busy cutting the green plants they will use in the winter.*
JEFF FOOTT

The curious communication of pikas

They live only in the rocky debris of mountain slopes, seldom venturing far from their rock shelters. Their voices are heard on any warm day, echoing around the rocks, sounding like shrill ventriloquists. Mouse-like ears and a foreshortened body give the creature the appearance of a stunted rat the size of your fist. But they are not rodents. They are pikas, also called conies, the smallest member of the rabbit family

Pikas have several communication signals. The most common is a warning call used for passing hawks, stalking coyotes, or sweating backpackers. A person can follow the path of a predator across a talus slope just by listening to the warning calls springing from the rocks near the prowling hunter. However, if a pika should be out in a meadow and a hawk passes over, it will dash for safety before giving the danger signal. Because the pika lives most of its life in the rocks or under the snow, few predators can snatch it before it darts away. However, weasels are slender and can follow pikas into their rock shelters. When a weasel is about, pikas are silent, hiding away quietly.

A colony of pikas has territorial signals, mating vocalizations, and other communications. Pairs of pikas sometimes signal together, like a duet. Even the young have two distinctive calls. Research has demonstrated varieties of signals between individuals and between colonies. Tape recordings of territorial calls from one area are not recognized by pikas from another area. Individual differences in signals may mean the pikas recognize each other's voices.

Should you pass a jumble of rocks and hear the squeaking cry of the pika, listen for the subtle differences in their voices and messages. Communication in the pika world is just beginning to be understood and translated. ▫

65

numbered in the hundreds of thousands, as many as a million or more. Nearly wiped out by market hunters, today's survivors are seldom related to the early Spanish mustang but are more likely the stock of a nearby ranch gone wild. Although their numbers have been reduced by public land managers, the Great Basin remains their stronghold.

The horses live in small bands dominated by a stallion. Tolerant of the arid Great Basin's heat and cold, the herds survive quite well, foraging over many miles of dry rangeland. Fights between competing stallions may last for days, leaving the loser exhausted and bleeding, sometimes fatally. One recent study of wild horses found 95 percent of adult males with visible scars, in part from the tendency of the animals to use their teeth, often in an attempt to sever the leg tendons of their opponents.

Many biologists regard the wild horse as a large, exotic creature asserting itself into a habitat at the expense of native species. For others, however, the sight of a band of horses fleeing across the sagebrush desert, dust swirling, the stallion protecting their flanks from all enemies, willing to fight until death if necessary, is a source of inspiration. On the public lands of the West, whether as a cultural symbol or source of inspiration, the wild horse belongs and is part of the western wildlife heritage.

If the horse is large and dominant, the graceful pronghorn antelope, now found in the northeastern corner of California, is the essence of speed. The pronghorn survives not by hiding but by virtue of its tremendous speed, up to sixty miles per hour. The fastest mammal in the western hemisphere, the antelope insists on living in open, grassy, sagebrush plains, where his keen eyes, which protrude like a rabbit's, can see in all directions. While walking it appears almost awkward, but once it begins to

run, there is no more graceful animal. At top speed it almost floats above the earth seemingly driven by the wind.

At one time pronghorns were found throughout the Central Valley and on the deserts of Southern California. Today they are confined largely to the public lands in the northeastern counties.

Biologically unique, they are the only member of their family. Unlike most animals with cousins or counterparts in similar environments around the world, the pronghorn is the only surviving species, one that dates back millions of years.

Except for mule deer, a few bighorn sheep that come out of the Sierra Nevada to winter on the slopes of the Great Basin, and the pronghorn, the region has no other large wildlife. In the air, the golden eagle can be seen, the largest and most powerful of the birds of prey. It may weigh up to twelve pounds and have a wingspan of seven feet. Unlike the bald

Above: *Wild horses— like this mare and her foal—evoke the spirit of the West more than any other animal. Today's herds of feral horses are greatly reduced from the one million or more that ranged the West early in this century.*
DAVID E. ROWLEY

Running with the wind

A country of wonderful contrasts, hot deserts bounded by snow-laden mountains, cinders and ashes scattered on glacier-polished pavement, frost and fire working together in the making of beauty.

—John Muir

East of the Sierra crest, in the rain shadow of its great bulk, lies the Great Basin. It is a land of sagebrush, pinyon pine, and long desert mountain ranges, "crawling like caterpillars toward the Gulf of Mexico," as one early geographer described the topography. Only a small area of California spills over the Sierra Nevada into the Great Basin, but this arid land supports a special community of plants and animals.

Depending on how the lines are drawn, there are at least three types of desert in California: the Mojave and Sonoran deserts of Southern California and the Great Basin Desert. Of these three types, the Great Basin is the coolest with frequent winter snow and north winds and the highest elevation. Sagebrush in the foothills and pinyon-juniper woodlands in the higher regions characterize its plant communities.

Geographically, the most unusual feature of the Great Basin is a series of closed valleys with no outlet to the sea. The Great Basin was once covered by large Pleistocene lakes, whose shorelines can easily be seen etched on the sides of many valleys. These inland seas have shrunk to a small fraction of their former size at Salt, Pyramid, Walker, and Mono lakes, yet they still influence the vegetation and wildlife of the basin.

The region was first crossed by the Spanish explorers Dominguez and Escalante in 1776. But it was to take another lifetime before John C. Fremont reported that a large closed basin of over 200,000 square miles lay in the American West.

Today, this region remains largely undeveloped and, with the exception of Reno, just east of the California border, sparsely populated. The drive south on Highway 395 from the Oregon line to the vague area where the Great Basin Desert merges with the Mojave remains one of the great scenic journeys in all the United States. The northeastern sagebrush environment covers 1.8 million acres of the state and pinyon-juniper woodland another 2.5 million acres. Throughout their range the two environments blend into each other, overshadowed and influenced by the Sierra Nevada to the west.

The mountains bring many natural forces to bear on their desert side, the most obvious of which is dryness. They wring most of the moisture from the Pacific air that sweeps from the west, then the dry winds pick up speed as they flow like water down the eastern slope.

Opposite: *Unlike the deer, the pronghorn, or American antelope, does not have the ability to leap, and its numbers have been reduced by the barbed wire fence.*
ROBERT WINSLOW

Right: *The western diamondback is the largest rattlesnake in the West and is regarded as one of the most dangerous of all North American serpents.*
MICHAEL CARDWELL

Late afternoon winds are common, bringing cold air from the high mountains and leaving frost on desert plants as late as June and as early as Labor Day. In the fall mule deer retreat down these eastern slopes to avoid the snow. In the spring the same snow, melted, flows into the basin to nurture riparian plants and wildlife as well as the dying desert lakes.

In this dry and corrugated landscape the largest wild animal and, for at least two decades, the most controversial is the wild horse. To the rancher they are hungry competitors with his cows for grass; to the urban tourist they represent a living symbol of the West; to public land managers they are a political headache. But to those who have seen the wild herds and witnessed the fierce battles between stallions, they are the wild essence of the Great Basin.

A distant cousin of the modern horse lived in the West until the late

Pleistocene when, along with many other large animals, they disappeared. Brought into the Southwest by Spanish pioneers, horses were adopted by the native Indians with fierce pride. At the turn of the century, wild horses

eagle, which is content to clean up a carcass or scavenge for food, the golden eagle is an active predator. A fierce and powerful hunter, it kills its prey with its long, sharp claws then tears the flesh with its hooked beak.

The golden eagle is widespread throughout the northern hemisphere and is the virile national symbol of both Mexico and Germany. Prized for falconry since the Middle Ages, its likeness is emblazoned on coins, coats of arms, and other emblems.

The eagle can also be seen in the coastal hills and mountains and less commonly in the Sierra Nevada. In the sagebrush country the eagle may laboriously take flight with a jackrabbit

in its claws, rising in front of your car like an apparition.

Like most birds of prey, the golden eagle takes many rabbits and rodents, and is essential to the balance of nature. However, to the sheepherder the bird is condemned because of its taste for fresh lamb. Even some sportsmen dislike the

Above left: *The rough-legged hawk is a rather gentle and unsuspicious predator. It often feeds on carrion, including ducks injured or killed by other means.*
FRANS LANTING

Above right: *A golden eagle feeds two of its young. The golden usually preys on rabbits and ground squirrels, unlike the bald eagle, which feeds on fish and carrion.*
TUPPER ANSEL BLAKE

creature because of its occasional predation on bighorn sheep lambs and young game species. Despite this, the bird is an exciting sight, casting an impressive shadow over a dry land.

A smaller, less controversial bird of the Great Basin is the chukar partridge. A native of southern Asia and the nations near the Mediterranean, the chukar was brought to California in 1932. Although it was introduced over much of the state by the Fish and Game Department, it flourished only in the high desert country.

The chukar is a pleasingly plump bird, nearly three times the size of a quail. Nesting and roosting on the ground, it lives in large coveys except during the nesting season. The females are ambitious, laying from seven to sixteen eggs. Although the young do not fly until they are two weeks old, the precocious birds leave the nest soon after hatching. The mother, like other ground-nesting birds, protects the young with her ability to act injured and lure away any predators.

The young feed on insects initially but eat

seeds, fruits, stems, and leaves of various plants. During the dry season they limit their range to within a mile of water; however, once it rains they scatter over a wide area.

Chukar coveys flush with a fast break when disturbed, then regroup with a clear ringing call. Although an introduced species, they fill a niche in the arid Great Basin, with no apparent harm to other species. To the birder and sportsman they are a welcome addition.

One native bird, recognized by even the most casual visitor to the pinyon-juniper forest, is the pinyon jay. With Clark's nutcracker and the scrub and Steller's jays also in evidence, raucous, brazen birds are common sights, each species preferring a slightly different habitat. The pinyon jay is a social, even gregarious bird, sometimes gathering in groups of several hundred.

When the seeds of the pinyon ripen in the fall, the lesser-known role of this bird becomes evident. Flocks of jays feed on the pinyon seeds, which they store in their flexible esophagi. The birds then carry the seeds, up to twenty per bird, to their nesting area, five or six miles away. The birds store the seeds by tucking them away under the ground litter of dead twigs and needles.

During the spring breeding season, males unearth the seeds as part of the courtship process. Nesting females and even the young, after they hatch, feed on the uncovered pine nuts stored from the fall before. Of course, many seeds are forgotten and germinate, eventually growing into mature trees.

Since the seed is large, it cannot be blown into new environments. If the seed merely falls from the tree, it lies on top of the ground and seldom takes root. Only the jay carries the seed to new environments and carefully tucks it into the ground for ideal growing conditions. The pinyon jay is a Johnny Pinyonseed of the Great Basin.

It is impossible to travel through the Great Basin, especially at night, and not be impressed by the number of jackrabbits this dry land supports. While the black-tailed species is found throughout most of California, the white-tailed jackrabbit lives only on the eastern edge of the state in the Great Basin. The largest of California's native hares, the white-tailed version weighs six to eight pounds and prefers life in these arid hills and mountains.

Like all members of this quiet and interesting family, the hares have many enemies: coyotes, bobcats, foxes, owls, hawks, and snakes. They maintain their numbers by growing up fast and breeding large families, up to eight young per litter. Like many animals in nature, their numbers rise and fall according to cycles and causes not fully understood. Their predators have their own cycles, usually lagging behind the hare's; the decline of the prey brings starvation to the predator.

Desert visitors are often impressed by the size of a jackrabbit's ears. Even from a distance they appear huge and almost glow with a pink translucence. The ears are believed to play an important role in cooling the body and vary in size according to the animal's normal habitat. The species with the largest ears is the desert-loving antelope jackrabbit, which has ears averaging over 23 percent of its body length. The black-tailed species has ears 20.7 percent of its length and still shorter in cooler climates. The white-tailed jackrabbit has ears approximately 18 percent of its length, and the snowshoe hare, living in colder climates, has ears 13 to 14 percent of its length and shorter in more northern and colder regions. Of course the little pika, living year-round in the alpine zone, has ears short and tidy like a mouse.

The bushy-tailed wood rat, common throughout the West, is found in the rimrock and rockslide areas of the Great Basin. Its most distinguishing feature, as its name implies, is its handsome squirrel-like tail. Called "pack rat" because of its habit of "trading" one object for another, it stores twigs, sticks, bones, food, and other material under logs or in rock crevices. Termed middens, these accumulations have been helpful to archaeologists.

Above: *The jackrabbit can see in nearly a complete circle with its bulging eyes. It often sits still and then, when startled, bounds up to twenty feet in a single leap.*
BARBARA BRUNDEGE

Opposite: *Each spring, 50,000 California gulls, 95 percent of the state's breeding population, nest at Mono Lake. In fall, the gulls scatter to coastal wintering areas.*
GALEN ROWELL

A mass of wood rat debris, which may include various animal droppings, tin cans, bottle tops, and other odds and ends a rat might encounter, is preserved by soaking with the animal's urine and body wastes. Portions of the midden become an encrusted mass and, if tucked away under a rock or in a cave, escape the elements and erosion. In this way, certain pack rat middens become mini-archaeological sites complete with samples of the resident bones and plant debris from thousands of years before, when the flora and fauna were quite different. In other words, the pack rat has become, in its own way, an archaeologist's assistant. One midden contained the tooth of an extinct camel, the jawbone of a long dead ground sloth, and bones of a condor that had spread its wings some 14,000 years before. So, on a camping trip, if a pack rat exchanges some useless item for your favorite spoon, just consider how fascinating it will be to a future archaeologist.

When it rains in the Great Basin or the snow of the Sierra Nevada melts, water flows into the nearly sterile alkaline valleys to the east. The water forms temporary ponds or lakes, and until it evaporates, the once large desert lakes can again be imagined. Centuries of evaporation have given these valleys such high concentrations of salts that plant and animal life is often impossible. But upstream there may be salt tolerant plants such as *Atriplex* and desert salt grass. One must travel even farther upstream to find the usual diversity of riparian wildlife that flourishes anywhere water flows through the dry California land.

Near Mono Lake you can see all these diverse habitats as well as the terraces of old Mono Lake, 600 or 700 feet above the present level. The lake itself, contrasting with the salt flats and more distant volcanic peaks, has been the scene of national environmental efforts. Its birds,

brine shrimp, and dropping water level have been the concern of conservationists. More recently, the lake was the focus of a landmark court decision that provided increased legal protection for Mono Lake and other public streams and lakes in the West.

During the year up to seventy-nine species of water birds, as well as almost every North American shorebird, duck, grebe, and gull species, visit the shores of Mono Lake. Five species—the California gull, snowy plover, northern and Wilson's phalaropes, and eared grebe—find the lake crucial to their survival. In recent years up to 50,000 California gulls, 95 percent of California's breeding pairs, nested at Mono Lake. For the thousands of birds migrating through this arid land, the water's prolific brine shrimp provide an important fueling stop.

Leaving the mysterious lake, traveling south on Highway 395, you pass through the pines at Mammoth Lake. The road drops into the Owens Valley, and ahead lies the salty bed of Owens Lake, dry now for sixty years to satisfy thirsty Los Angeles. As you continue south, the road drops lower, and the Great Basin Desert merges into the brilliant and dry Mojave. ■

The Desert Rat

On the dry lands of California live fifteen different species of kangaroo rat *(Dipodomys sp.)*. In all the major desert areas of the world—Africa, Asia, Australia, and the western United States—a similar but unrelated type of desert rodent is found. Somehow these rodents, sharing similar habits and appearances, evolved independently of each other in the desert environment. All can survive on little or no water.

The kangaroo rat lives without any water, instead producing its own from dry vegetation. Oxidation of food, however, yields only a small amount of water. The animal's secret is its kidney, which is four times as efficient as a human's and can excrete urine twice as salty as sea water. The kangaroo rat is the only mammal known to drink sea water and safely excrete the salt. Other mammals find salt water fatal.

To further reduce water loss from its body, the rat has adopted a nocturnal life style, staying in its underground tunnel when the humidity is lowest and the temperature highest outside. At night when the temperature has moderated and the humidity rises, the kangaroo rat comes out to feed. And if there should be a rare desert rainstorm, he doesn't even bother to have a drink. ■

Desert Pupfish

The hottest valley in North America, named simply Death Valley, still has water. The driest deserts in California have a few scattered permanent springs of water. These are usually warm in temperature and often as salty as seawater. Stand next to a shallow trickle of desert water, watch as it emerges from a rock

crevice and sinks into the desert within a few hundred yards. It is hard to imagine, but such water is a tenuous relic of the great Pleistocene lakes and rivers that once existed here.

Many of these desert springs are home to the desert pupfish. Although isolated 10,000 to 30,000 years ago by the drying of the Great Basin, these tiny half-inch-long fish share a common family background. There are twenty distinct populations of the pupfish in 3,000 square miles of desert around Death Valley.

A few years ago after several populations were exterminated, the pupfish became the object of research for the first time. It was discovered that the fish have the ability to tolerate, in a short time period, water temperature changes of 70 degrees Fahrenheit. Most fish have a much narrower temperature-range tolerance. Forty degrees is common, and many tropical species have even more restrictions on their water temperatures. Pupfish also have the ability to adjust to changing water salinity, a critical adaption

where seasonal flows vary so much.

Small desert fish, isolated in one of the world's harshest environments, have adapted and survived for thousands of years. While their biology is complex and the physiological processes important, desert pupfish may be most worthwhile as a source of human inspiration. They seem fragile but are some of the toughest and most adaptable fish anywhere.

William Beebe wrote in 1906 the best summary of the consequences of extinction: "The beauty and genius of a work of art may be reconceived, though its first material expression be destroyed: a vanished harmony may yet again inspire the composer: but when

the last individual of a race of living things breathes no more, another heaven and earth must pass before such a one can be again." ■

Above left: *The Merriam kangaroo rat may look awkward, but its long, powerful hind legs help it make spectacular leaps.*
TUPPER ANSEL BLAKE
Above right: *Salt, not snow, surrounds the trickle of warm, salty water that is the habitat of a school of Death Valley pupfish.*
TUPPER ANSEL BLAKE
Right: *There are now five species of pupfish found in Death Valley.*
TUPPER ANSEL BLAKE

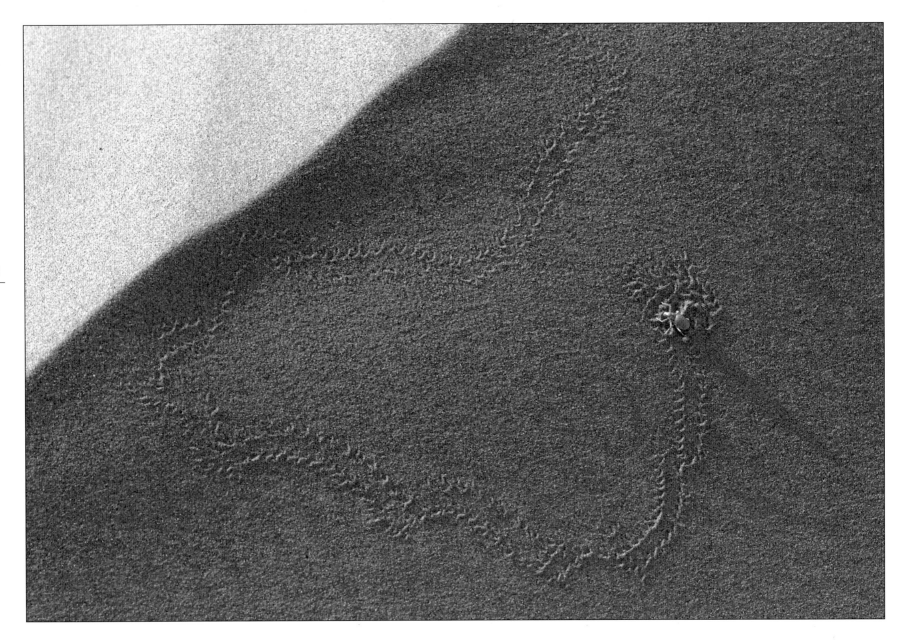

A place in the sun

This is the sense of the desert hills, that there is room enough and time enough.

—Mary Austin

For the uninitiated, deserts are a barren land, mysterious, threatening, and seemingly lifeless. The Southern California deserts are no exception. Lying east of the coastal and Sierra Nevada ranges, they are in the rain shadow of the winds that flow from the Pacific. Sparse moisture means few plants, and those that survive are tough, with defensive mechanisms like thorns or spines. If you are new to the desert, wildlife seems scarce as well. However, if you are near a spring, a small seep, or any water as the sun drops to the west, the desert comes alive with wildlife.

Like the plants that have adapted to the harsh land and harsher sun, wildlife has also adapted to the desert environment. The first law of survival here is to avoid the sun and heat. Millions of desert recreationists have responded much the same way. Visit Death Valley or any other California desert region in the hot summer, which begins in May, and few people will be about. You will find an empty land, some of the most isolated geography in the United States. Return in the winter or spring, and the desert throbs with activity in Death Valley, Joshua Tree National Monument, and Anza-Borrego Desert State Park. Campers and hikers come by the thousands and find a surprisingly gentle desert, one with many wild residents, if you know where to find them.

A good place to discover wildlife is in one of the desert's sand dune areas. On any morning hike you will find the story of the night's activity written on the sand. Many burrows have busy trails leading out to all points on the compass, others have damp sand thrown up from below. Closer viewing reveals the tracks of pocket mice, the larger tracks of a kangaroo rat, and perhaps a trace where its long tail brushed the sand. Often the tracks of a coyote or bobcat show where they searched from hole to hole in the sand. Occasionally, you find the brush marks of an owl wing or the bloody remnants of a successful hunt.

Armed with a field guide to animal tracks and a curiosity about the land and its creatures, you will be on your way to discovering the desert's special wild community. Unlike the more complex and moist environments, the ecology of the desert is relatively open, simple, and easy to decipher.

If the desert sands are useful to understand the wildlife, they can also confuse. The track of the sidewinder rattlesnake, for example, the result of a looping sideways movement of its coils, leaves a peculiar mark. The snake's skating motion permits it to grip the sand more efficiently and travel faster in pursuit of its prey.

Opposite: *Desert sand holds the story of a wandering gray snout beetle. Sand dunes provide the best place to observe the tracks of wildlife.*
MICHAEL S. SAMPLE

Right: *The bold roadrunner is synonymous with the desert of the Southwest. Its distinctive track has two toes facing forward and two facing backward.*
D. CAVAGNARO

Still another adaptation of the sidewinder is a pair of "horns" that fold down to protect its eyes from sand when it is in a burrow. The sidewinder is small, only eighteen inches to two feet long, and travels the dunes in search of mice or kangaroo rats. Like the kingsnake, the sidewinder also eats other snakes.

Honey and screw-bean mesquite trees often stabilize the dunes, as do other trees such as the catclaw, tamarisk, and several types of shrubs. These areas attract wildlife for shelter, shade, or food. Below the surface the roots provide a framework that keeps rodent tunnels from collapsing. Larger burrows may have been made by the desert cottontail, which often adopts smaller rodent burrows and enlarges them for its own use.

The distant cousin of the cottontail, the black-tailed jackrabbit, does not burrow but merely huddles under a shrub or tree in the shade and clears out a slight depression or "form" in the sand. One of the most familiar animals of the West and Southwest, this hare is noted for its bounding gait, reaching speeds up to thirty-five miles per hour. It survives in the desert in part due to its precocious young. They are capable of hopping and escaping some predators at birth. It breeds year-round and has up to seven young per litter. The young are often the target of snakes as well as hawks. The mature animals are a staple of coyotes, bobcats, owls, and golden eagles.

During the day, even in the desert sun, you may see lizards darting from bush to bush for shade. On the fine sand their tracks may be small and numerous. Occasionally their whip-like tails lash the sand, leaving a clue as to the owners of the tracks. The lizards reflect more adaptations to the desert. The fringe-toed lizard has projecting scales on its hind toes which help provide traction in the sand. Its flattened body, receding jaw, nasal valves, and ear flaps help it plunge into loose sand and "swim" under it. Like the sidewinder, its eyes are protected from the sand as are its lungs. In this way it escapes both the hot sun and its predators. This lizard can also rise up on its hind legs and sprint across the desert floor to minimize the heat gain.

This ability is important to protect the lizard from hot temperatures. The desert spiny lizard, for example, found near the Colorado River, cannot tolerate a body temperature above 109 degrees Fahrenheit. Yet reptiles character-istically have a variable body temperature, usually slightly higher than the air temperature. This condition, called poikilothermic or being "cold-blooded," is energy efficient. Instead of maintaining a constant warm temperature like mammals, a reptile's temperature and meta-bolic rate are lower during the cool season, making fewer demands on the animal. Nevertheless, reptiles run the risk of fatally high temperatures in the desert. Most desert snakes cannot tolerate body temperatures above 110 degrees Fahrenheit and must avoid the direct sun during the summer months.

The desert is defined by its dryness, and many animals have adapted to both the dryness

and heat. But twice a year, rain activates those creatures that took another path of adaptation. In the fall the Pacific storm tracks begin to move south along the western coast of North America. By late fall of most years, they periodically push onto the Southern California shore. Depending on their strength and persistence, the storms penetrate the coastal range and bring gentle

rains that may last for several days to the desert valleys.

The second type of moisture comes in the summer and is known for its intensity and brevity. During the summer months when the Pacific storm track is far north, warm and very moist tropical air sometimes invades the southwestern deserts. Its pattern is to charge north out of the Gulf of Mexico then hook left or westward across the southwest. Its frequency decreases from east to west. Southeastern Arizona receives many more storms than the southwestern deserts of Arizona and California near the Colorado River. Nevertheless, most years, several of these masses of tropical air arrive, colliding

Above: *The cottontail is one of the most common desert animals. Although most active at night, it can also be seen in late afternoon or on rare cool days.* TED LEVIN

Opposite: *A black, wedge-shaped mark on the neck identifies this creature as the desert spiny lizard. A good climber, this lizard feeds on insects and seeks shelter in crevices.* TED LEVIN

with the dry northern air to create violent thunderstorms with brief, intense rainfall.

Following the footprint of these storms, some unlikely creatures emerge for another cycle of activity and regeneration. Among these are members of the amphibian family, whose dual lives, first as aquatics then as terrestrials, seem impossible in the dry land. The spadefoot toad, taking advantage of temporary ponds and moisture, accelerates its life cycle and emerges following these storms, equipped with a loud voice designed to quickly bring the opposite sexes together. Sometimes only an hour after the first heavy desert rain in months, the night comes alive with their urgent voices. With what appears as undue haste, the toads mate and produce eggs. Within nine to seventy-two hours, the eggs become tadpoles. In a race against the drying sun and fleeting nature of desert ponds, the tadpoles reach maturity in twelve to forty days.

The adult then retreats into a rodent hole or burrows into the moist soil with a spade-like projection on its hind foot. The toad turns and backs into its burrow, grinding a hole much like a person steps on a cigarette. There it waits until the next year. If the desert rains fail to arrive, it may wait a second year. As further protection against dehydration, it produces several layers of skin that are loosened from its body but aren't completely sloughed off in the burrows. This covering helps to conserve water and reduce evaporation.

Desert toads and frogs bring other adaptations to this harsh land as well. Like many of the desert-dwelling mammals, they are usually nocturnal. The Great Plains toad stores up to 30 percent of its body weight as water. Some species have a seat patch like a wick to absorb moisture from the ground. Others can, in the tadpole stage, tolerate the high temperatures of a desert pond as well as salty water. Unlike mammals, the amphibians can tolerate up to 60

percent dehydration and still survive. All add to the diversity of desert wildlife.

One of the most conspicuous predators of the desert's lizards and snakes is the roadrunner. No other bird has captured the public's imagination the way this one has. The size of a small chicken, the roadrunner is fast, has an expressive tail, and seems comical. Little wonder it became a mainstay of cartoons and postcards. But the roadrunner is a quick and deadly killer. Its strong beak acts like a small sword, skewering its prey. Not to be outdone, some lizards have a breakaway tail, which separates from the body when grabbed, leaving the roadrunner with a twitching morsel but hardly a full meal. Later the lizard's tail is regenerated.

A member of the cuckoo family, the roadrunner is most common to the deserts, although it is also found in the Central Valley north to Redding and occasionally in the foothill and chaparral environments. Its track is unique with two toes forward and two backward, making a distinctive "X" shape. The roadrunner can fly,

Above: *A Jerusalem cricket is wingless, clumsy, and harmless. It scavenges at night on dead animals and plants and usually hides under cover during the day.*
MARK J. RAUZON

Opposite: *Few places in the United States offer the solitude and wild emptiness of the California desert. It is a harsh land, but a region rich in wildlife and diversity.*
TUPPER ANSEL BLAKE

but it is usually seen walking or running.

The roadrunner is omnivorous, and its appetite voracious. It eats not just lizards and snakes but also seeds, fruits, and small birds and mammals. In the past it has been persecuted for eating quail eggs, but research has shown eggs to be a small part of its diet. Today, it is one of the most welcome desert birds.

The Gambel's quail, traveling from bush to bush in bursts of nervous and disorganized energy, is another symbol of the desert. On almost any morning a desert camper awakens to the rallying call of a quail drawing the flock together. With a topknot dangling over its head, the Gambel's quail, like the roadrunner, is almost a desert trademark.

The Gambel's, mountain, and California quails are all chicken-like, or gallinaceous, birds. As such they spend most of their time on the ground scratching for food. At night they perch in bushes or trees for protection from predators. During the fall and winter they form coveys, but they pair up in the spring for nesting. At one time the birds were a staple of market hunters. In the late nineteenth century quail was a regular item on restaurant menus. Habitat changes, overgrazing, and agriculture have reduced their numbers. Where conditions are favorable, the birds respond quickly and dramatically to management improvements. Because they depend on water, over 3,000 gallinaceous guzzlers, specially designed bird-watering devices, have been installed by the Fish and Game Department to encourage their development.

The Joshua tree, with its contorted and ungainly limbs, dominates the Mojave Desert at elevations from 2,500 to 5,000 feet in Southern California. The "tree" is more accurately a lily, but it has a woody trunk and reaches over twenty-five feet high. It provides food and shelter for many different kinds of

peckers for nesting sites. Once abandoned, these ready-made holes become homes for house wrens, ash-throated flycatchers, sparrow hawks, and others.

The Yucca night lizard, less than two inches long with a velvet-like skin, has evolved into a niche created by the Joshua tree. Offering shade from the sun, cover from predators, and food in the insects it attracts, the Joshua tree provides an ideal habitat for the tiny lizard. While it may be found elsewhere, it prefers life in the debris that accumulates under the gangly desert tree.

Other animals associated with the Joshua tree are the western toad, red-spotted toad, California treefrog, and Pacific treefrog. Also found are the banded gecko, chuckwalla, collared, leopard, zebra-tailed, desert spiny, side-blotched, night, whiptail, and desert horned lizards. Among the mammals are four bats, two rabbits, two ground squirrels, three pocket mice, three moles, two rats, two foxes, as well as the raccoon, badger, bobcat, and mountain sheep, all with a preference for Joshua trees.

A unique feature of the California desert is the largest native palm tree found in the United States, the desert fan palm *(Washingtonia filifera)*. Located near springs, seeps, or periodic streams, the fan palm is a special surprise in the desert because of its size, up to seventy-five feet high, and the great mixture of life it attracts. Tucked away in canyons and remote areas, fan palm oases appear like tropical islands in the

Above: *In summer, tarantulas can be seen crossing quiet desert backcountry roads. Despite their lethal image, tarantulas are harmless.*
BARBARA BRUNDEGE AND EUGENE FISHER

Opposite: *Desert bighorn sheep have an impressive ability to move over rugged mountains. The male's large horns grow each year until they coil into a full circle.*
RON SANFORD

brilliant desert light.

More than eighty species of birds use the palms at one time or another during the year. Birdwatchers have been surprised to see American avocets, belted kingfishers, and even migrating snow geese rise from the trees. Some two dozen bird species nest in and around the palms, whose dry fronds make excellent cover. These include mourning doves, owls, roadrunners, and house finches. The brilliant hooded oriole uses palm fibers for its basket-like nest, which it attaches to the underside of the palm leaf.

The only place the western yellow bat has been sighted in California has been in and around the fan palms.

Scientists have been puzzled by the scattered location of the palms. How are the seeds dispersed? Are the palms relics of an earlier, moister era? The answer seems to lie in its fruit.

A mature palm produces up to 500,000 fruits each fall. Pea sized, the fruits have a sweet flesh similar to commercial dates. The seed is relatively large and rock-hard. Birds such as the western bluebird and cedar waxwing strip the fruit from but do not eat the tough seed. Laboratory studies found that the cactus mouse and antelope ground squirrel also eat the fruit but not the seed.

However, it was discovered that the coyote gorges itself on palm fruits. As the animal digests the fruit, the seeds pass through its body. During the fall, a coyote scat may contain hundreds of palm seeds. These seeds not only are still viable but germinate with twice the success of unprocessed seeds. Further research revealed that the seeds stay inside the coyote's intestine up to three days, a period which allows it to travel as far as thirty-six miles. The likely dispersal agent for the fan palm was found, the wily coyote.

One large native mammal found in the desert

wildlife. At least twenty-five bird species nest in the Joshua tree, and another twenty-five bird species are associated with it, as are twenty-five reptile, twenty-eight mammal, and four amphibian species.

Joshua tree "forests" are usually found on gravelly desert mountain slopes that are higher, cooler, and somewhat less harsh than the lower, hotter Sonoran Desert environment. They receive more moisture, including some winter snow. Nevertheless, the plants and their associated animals can withstand prolonged drought, heat, and persistent winds.

The inner pith of the Joshua tree is easily drilled by flickers and ladder-backed wood-

82

reduces competition. Since 1975 the desert bighorn has increased over much of its native range in the Southwest from 9,000 animals to over 15,000. The critical factor is often improving water supplies, for the animal needs to drink every few days, especially in the summer. The young are especially vulnerable, not just to predators but to stress brought on by cattle, people, or feral burros at the water holes.

Feral burros, aggressive, intelligent, and tough, are common in Death Valley and other desert areas. The animals, abandoned by prospectors or ranchers, have thrived in the region. Burros are especially damaging to springs and water sources critical not only to bighorns but other desert natives as well. Attempts by land managers to fence off springs and protect them from burros are often futile, as the animals push over the fences and trample the springs.

In parts of Death Valley, burros are overly friendly, not unlike the beggar bears once found in Yellowstone. Stop your car, roll down the window, and a burro is likely to stick its head in to look for apples, fruit, or anything edible.

In recent years federal agencies have attempted to eliminate burros from such areas as the Grand Canyon or to reduce their numbers to lessen the competition with bighorns or cattle. Many are trapped each year and offered for adoption as pets. Given the attractiveness of the animal, its adaptability and survivability, it will persist in the California desert for many years to come. ∎

country always attracts a great deal of interest, the diminutive desert bighorn sheep. Relatively small, only thirty to thirty-nine inches at the shoulder with an average weight of 160 pounds for males and a little over 100 pounds for females, it is the most difficult sheep for hunters after the "Grand Slam," the popular hunting goal, to legally possess.

The desert bighorn sheep, like many large western mammals, went into a sharp decline from 1850 to 1900. Isolated populations of bighorn sheep were completely eliminated from many desert ranges. Disease from domestic sheep, livestock competition for forage and water, and market hunting extirpated the animal from much of its territory.

Sheep have been reintroduced into many of their old desert ranges through trap and transplant programs. Management of domestic livestock has improved in some areas, which

Above: *The tracks of a coyote—along with its nighttime songs—are part of the mystery of California wildlife. Tracks are tangible clues to the wildlife saga in any area.*
PATRICK CONE

Opposite: *An ancient symbol of the California desert is the gentle desert tortoise. Although it asks very little from the land, the tortoise is now an endangered species.*
TED LEVIN

Desert tortoise

At first glance the desert tortoise *(Gopherus agassizi)* seems an unlikely creature to generate strong feelings. It is neither handsome nor swift, does nothing to antagonize anyone, and requires little from its environment. Until man and his machines, it wandered the deserts like a lonely prophet, with few enemies and no particular friends. Today, a discussion of the California desert, livestock grazing, or off-road vehicles is incomplete without mention of the desert tortoise.

The tortoise lives fifty to one hundred years under normal conditions, taking fifteen to twenty years to reach sexual maturity. Distinguished by being the largest reptilian herbivore in California, there is growing concern over its fate.

The tortoise is collected by those wanting to take it back home for a "pet," crushed under the wheels of off-road vehicles, and shot by vandals for entertainment. It is too hopelessly slow and ponderous to be able to locate enough food after its desert habitat has been stripped of vegetation by cattle. When stressed by poor nutrition, the female may not lay her eggs, bringing further declines to the population. After laborious digging, tortoises' shallow burrows are frequently trampled by cattle or sheep, especially during the summer. The slow-moving animals, once their shelter from the hot sun is crushed, may die from overheating before they can dig a new one.

Now proposed for listing as an endangered species, tortoise conservation efforts are opposed by unsympathetic land managers and those users of the public land who fear burdensome regulations. But many others are finding the animal a fascinating example of desert adaptation. Like other declining species, it serves as a warning light, or miner's canary, that all is not well with the western land. ∎

Giants of the deep

On all these shores there are echoes of past and future: of the flow of time, obliterating yet containing all that has gone before; of the seas' eternal rhythms—the tides, the beat of surf, the pressing rivers of the currents—shaping, changing, dominating; of the stream of life, flowing as inexorably as any ocean current, from past to unknown future.

—Rachel Carson, *The Edge of the Sea*

On the sunset edge of California lies an 800-mile coastal zone where the timeless sea meets a restless continental plate. In this region of earthquakes and tides, life from two worlds clash, one fresh and familiar, the other mysterious and alien.

At this interface the first explorers encountered California, with its great bears feeding on beached whales and cool fogs shrouding brown hills. The hills hid a great valley teeming with waterfowl, and still more hills, holding great oaks, led to John Muir's "mountain range of light." It was a rugged and uninviting coast, with few beaches and fewer harbors, except for one world-class harbor that lay hidden in fog from those early explorers.

In the sea, then as now, were large and impressive marine mammals. Each winter warm coves and lagoons along the Baja Coast attracted forty-five-foot whales for a passive nursery. Today, from March to May, some 13,000 gray whales and their young trek up the California Coast for the summer feeding grounds in the Bering Sea. Every fall the pregnant females leave the Bering Sea to start the migration south, where their route takes them within 400 feet of California at many points. Passing in the fog, sometimes within sound of California's morning commute, they quietly persist in the longest migration of any mammal.

Moving at a leisurely seven or eight knots, the magnificent animals, weighing up to 40,000 pounds, are visible from the coast, thrilling observers on Highway 1 in Big Sur, at Point Reyes, and many other viewpoints. Thousands take whale-watching boat trips off the coast to get a closer look at the friendly beasts. Now protected from whaling, gray whales are expanding their numbers after being once reduced to near extinction.

At times whales are irritated by barnacles on their skin, whale lice, lamprey eels, and other pests. They rub on rocks or on the sandy ocean bottom. Out of irritation, confusion, or perhaps curiosity, they leave their migration route. In October and November of 1985, Californians and much of the nation followed "Humphrey," a humpback whale, up the Sacramento River to almost within sight of the state capitol. A massive rescue effort was launched to shepherd Humphrey back down the river, through the San Francisco Bay, and out the Golden Gate to the Pacific. Finally, after reaching a shallow slough, the forty-foot, four-ton whale was led, or chased, downriver to the sea.

Whales are insulated by a thick layer of fat, or blubber, which also provides energy reserves for their long migrations. Essential to young whales for growth and high energy is the fat in their mothers' milk. Human milk has 2 percent fat, cow's milk has 4 percent fat, but baby whales drink milk averaging 40 percent fat.

The blue whale, occasionally seen on the California Coast, doubles the weight of its baby within the first week of birth on a diet of rich milk. A human baby takes six months to accomplish the same growth. Furthermore, the blue whale baby, which weighs two tons at birth and four tons in a week, grows to twenty to twenty-three tons after six or seven months. Reaching a length of one hundred feet and a weight of one hundred tons, the blue whale is the largest animal known to exist, including extinct dinosaurs.

The gray, blue, and humpback whales are three of the seven baleen-type whales that visit

Opposite: *California sea lions can frequently be seen sunning on rocks and bell buoys. In the water, sea lions are effective predators, feeding on salmon and steelhead.*
RICHARD HERRMANN

Right: *The striking tufted puffin is one of the tamest of the coastal birds. Its bill, small and dull brown in winter, during the breeding season grows large and bright.*
JEFF FOOTT

the coast of the state. The baleen whale does not have teeth but strains seawater through the sheets of baleen that hang from the roof of its mouth to filter out krill and other small organisms. In this way some of the sea's smallest animals sustain the largest.

The right whale, an occasional visitor to the West Coast, has been known to dive and stay down for eighty minutes, although most whales stay down for much shorter periods. Several factors combine to permit such long diving times. Most land mammals fill only 10 to 20 percent of their lungs with each breath, but whales exchange 80 to 90 percent of their capacity. The basal metabolic rate of whales is only one-fifteenth that of man, and their blood can hold enough oxygen to maintain this rate for an hour. When diving, whales, as well as dolphins and seals, lower their normal heart rate by half. Whales also have the ability to constrict the flow of blood to nonessential areas of the body, such as the intestines, while maintaining a flow to vital organs.

Other marine mammals found in California waters are dolphins and porpoises. The common dolphin, depicted in art for thousands of years, is well-known for its habit of running with ships and leaping from the water. Unfortunately, the nets of fishermen capture this lively creature, and it often suffocates before it can be released.

The Pacific white-sided dolphin sometimes travels in large schools up to a thousand. An animal that adapts well to confinement and training, it is the dolphin often exhibited in Marineland zoos and exhibitions.

Two porpoises are found in the state's waters, the harbor variety, seen in bays and harbors, and the chunky but striking black-and-white Dall porpoise.

Largest of the dolphin family is the well-known killer whale, or orca. Although a savage

predator of seals, walruses, and other dolphins as well as fish and squid, the orca does not usually bother boats or even kayakers. Eskimos, however, have as part of their oral history stories about killer whales attacking humans. Apparently, they hunt under ice floes to knock resting seals into the water. A human shadow, filtered through the Arctic ice may well resemble a tasty seal. Skin divers on the California Coast have encountered orcas on many occasions without being attacked.

Moving from the sea to the rugged islands and coastline of California brings a different mix of wildlife, including eared seals, fur seals, sea lions, and hair seals.

Rarest is the Guadalupe fur seal. Once common on the Farallon Islands off San Francisco, this seal was driven to the edge of extinction. In recent decades their numbers have increased, but they normally remain confined to off-shore islands.

The northern, or Alaska, fur seal, the best-

Opposite: *A bull elephant seal, weighing up to 8,000 pounds, shows off his snout.*
JACK D. SWENSON
Above left: *The salt harvest mouse, seen here in its native environment, is now an* endangered species.
JEFF FOOTT
Above right: *Rescue personnel on the California Coast are important to the protection of many wildlife species.*
FRANK S. BALTHIS

known seal in the world, congregates now on breeding rookeries where once it was hunted nearly to extinction. Like most wildlife, protection and good management have increased its numbers from a low of approximately 100,000 to two million or more today. Breeding in the north, they are seen off the California Coast but seldom come ashore.

Sea lions use off-shore islands, rocky points, and isolated beaches for haul out areas for rest and sleep. Both the California and Steller sea lions can be seen on Seal Rock near the Cliff House in San Francisco and many other observation points along the coast. The California sea lion is the smaller of the two—a male tips

88

the scales at 500 to 1,000 pounds and the female's weight ranges from 200 to 600 pounds. The California variety, noted for its continual honking bark, is the typical circus "seal."

The northern, or Steller, sea lion, is nearly twice as long as the California model and weighs 1,500 to 2,000 pounds. The Steller's coat is a tawny, yellowish brown compared with the rich, dark brown of the smaller species.

The annual summer breeding season brings bedlam to the traditional mating grounds. Males battle each other and struggle to hold together harems of ten to twenty females, remaining on the breeding grounds for two months without food. Only a few days after the

birth of the pups, the struggle for harems begins. The constant din from the crowded seals and sea lions bleating and challenging each other overwhelms the area. At Año Nuevo State Reserve, the largest breeding grounds of the Steller, over 2,000 animals have been counted on the beaches in recent years. Mortality among the new pups reaches as high

as 50 percent as the young are often crushed in the confusion and struggle.

Sea lions were once hunted for their hides, oil, and fur. In the nineteenth century, many of the species seen off the California Coast were close to extinction. In 1927, the California sea lion was estimated to total less than 1,000, but its numbers are now believed to be nearly 50,000, a remarkable recovery.

Some fishermen dislike sea lions because of the damage they cause to nets and their predation on fish. However, research has shown that the sea lion's diet consists largely of squid, octopus, and rough fish that have little commercial value. Today it is clear that man and marine wildlife can co-exist to the benefit of both.

Unlike sea lions and fur seals, which can travel on their flippers while on land, hair seals are unable to move their hind flippers forward and can only wriggle. Three types of hair seals have been found on the California Coast: the ribbon seal, harbor seal, and elephant seal.

The rarest species is the ribbon seal. Normally found on the coast of Alaska, and even there rarely, one animal was lassoed from the sea by a cowboy and pulled ashore near Morro Bay in November of 1962. Positive identification was made at nearby California Polytechnic State University.

More common is the small harbor seal, whose mottled coat has earned it the nickname "spotted" seal. Often seen in San Francisco Bay, they sometimes travel miles upstream into freshwater regions, where they may pull themselves onto inland docks to sun and please passing boaters. Seldom venturing far off the coast, this quiet, peaceful animal is usually found singly or in small groups.

Named for its odd, inflatable proboscis, the elephant seal is California's largest. Males are unlikely looking creatures reaching seventeen

Above: *A red bill, pink legs, and yellow eyes are distinguishing characteristics of the American black oystercatcher. It is usually seen feeding near rocks.*
MIKE DANZENBAKER

Opposite: *Sand and tide, wind and waves: all bring beauty to the California Coast. The next storm may shatter this intricate shell, reducing its fragments into minerals.*
FRANK S. BALTHIS

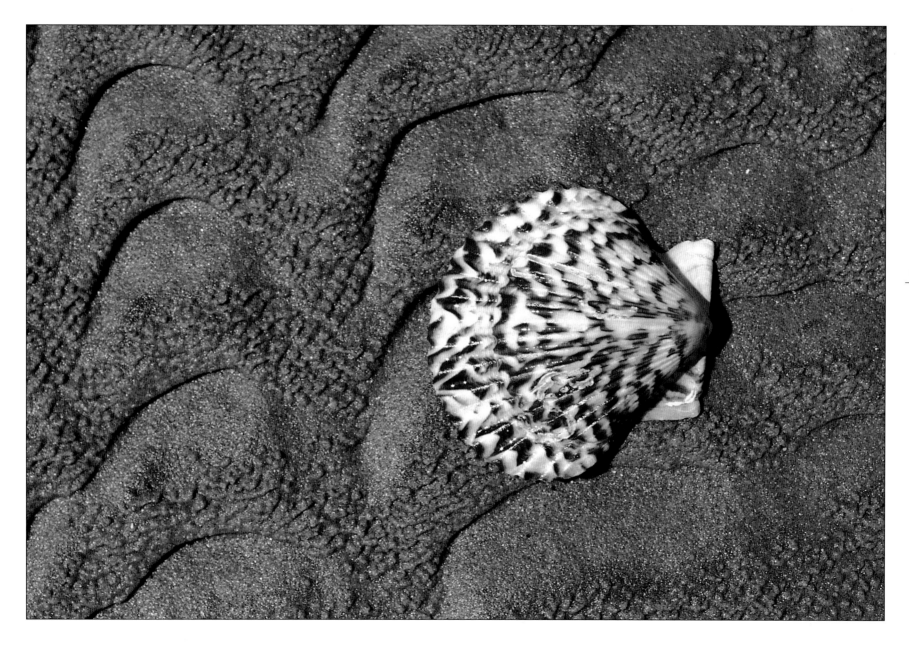

feet long and weighing a fleshy 5,000 pounds. The nose is normally relaxed and hangs over the bull's mouth, except during mating season when it is inflated. Then the organ quivers and bends down to lie against the roof of the mouth and pharynx. The bull produces sound not by its vocal chords but by bursts of snorts through the proboscis.

The bulls fight awkwardly, traveling slowly across the beaches with a blubbery, undulating motion, ignoring the pups born a few weeks before and sometimes crushing them. Compared to the two-and-a-half-ton males, the females, only half as long and weighing 1,700 pounds, seem almost dainty.

Usually eight to forty females make up a harem, which the bull protects from other intruding males. Despite their carelessness, the bulls do not intentionally injure others. Sea lions may romp over them and even sleep on them during cold weather, sharing the heat radiating from their considerable bulk.

The elephant seal's comeback from the brink of extinction in the 1800s is a noteworthy

Above: *The abundant resources of the California Coast attract clam diggers today just as they have for thousands of years.*
PATRICK CONE
Opposite: *Few wildlife environments contrast* *more sharply than at the coast. These rookeries escape the highest tides, while nearby tidepools expose a rich diversity of aquatic life at low tide.*
JEFF FOOTT

conservation saga. For forty years, seal oil was a mainstay for home and street lighting, lubricating machinery, and making paint and soap. Since a large bull yielded over 200 gallons of oil, the animals were highly sought after.

By 1860 their numbers were so reduced that commercial hunting was no longer worthwhile, and in 1869 the elephant seal was commonly considered extinct. Several museums sent expeditions in the 1880s into the old ranges from Alaska to Baja, but it was not until 1892 that a Smithsonian Institution expedition found eight elephant seals on a volcanic island off the coast of Baja. The museum collectors promptly killed seven of the seals, knowing they were "the last of an exceedingly rare species."

The population at that point was probably less than a hundred animals and perhaps as few as twenty. In 1922 the Mexican government gave formal protection to the species, and by the 1930s they began to appear once again on the California Coast. In the early 1960s Año Nuevo hosted over 400 elephant seals each year. Today at least twelve colonies exist on the California and Baja coast with a population in excess of 60,000 animals.

If the elephant seal is one of nature's homeliest animals, the sea otter is one of the most handsome. Playful, athletic, and energetic, they endear themselves to most who see them.

Native Indians cherished their furs, and as early as 1700 their lush, silken hides were prized by the elite of Asia. Fortunes were made trading and selling sea otter furs. It was the sea otter that brought the Russian empire into Alaska and down the coast to California. The sea otter trade challenged the Spanish empire's tenuous hold on California and lured aggressive Yankee traders to the region. In one sense the handsome sea otter was part of

America's Manifest Destiny.

Commerce led to the sea otter's decline. Unlike those mammals sought for their blubber, the otter compensates for its lack of fat by producing a superior fur coat, glossy, soft, dense, and unexcelled in nature. Even early in this century, single fine sea otter skins were sold for over $1,000 each.

From 1741 to 1911 over a million sea otters were harvested. Finally in 1911 a treaty to protect the sea otter was signed. Two years later California gave additional protection to those on its coast.

Complete protection led to their revival. In 1938 after they were feared extinct on the California Coast, a herd of approximately fifty was photographed fifteen miles south of Carmel. The recovery of the most appealing of all marine mammals had begun.

Today fishing nets, rifles, pollution, and oil all imperil the sea otter. Other than man, the only predator of any consequence to the animal is the orca.

A member of the weasel family and related to the river otter, the sea otter has a flattened tail, large webbed hind feet, and a limber body that enables it to swim with great skill. Males measure up to four and a half feet long and can weigh up to eighty pounds. Females seldom exceed forty-five pounds.

Spending most of its time in the water, the sea otter depends on kelp beds. It can often be seen on the kelp resting or feeding on its back or cleaning its sleek fur to protect it from hypothermia. Otters dive to the bottom as deep as 180 feet to locate prey. Their diet consists largely of sea urchins, mussels, shellfish, and octopus, but they also feed on abalone, which has earned them the hostility of some fishermen. Fishermen, in fact, have been major opponents of expanding the range of the otter.

Interestingly, the sea otter is one of the few

9 1

animals in nature to use a tool. After bringing a mussel or other shellfish to the surface, the otter, lying on its back, holds a rock on its chest and beats the mussel on the rock. Individuals have been seen using a Coke bottle instead of a rock. People walking near the rugged coast are often startled by the pounding sound, carried across the surface and kelp beds to the shore. Careful observation reveals an otter on its back intently working on opening its latest meal.

At one time the northern and southern herds were continuous wherever there were beds of kelp. The southern herd once ranged from the Farallon Islands south to Baja. The northern herd was distributed from the Aleutian Islands into Russian and Japanese waters with a population in excess of 100,000. Today the southern herd, which numbers about 1,600, is listed as threatened and is concentrated on the Big Sur Coast. In the fall of 1987, the first of 250 otters, mostly young, were reintroduced into the Channel Islands, sixty miles west of Los Angeles. If this second population is successful, it will reduce the risk of the southern herd's being wiped out by an oil spill or other disaster.

A stunning variety of invertebrates flourishes in the intertidal zone, that area between the land and sea which is alternately covered and exposed by the changing tides. Animals living there must hold their niche with tenacious determination.

It is not unusual for an inventory of invertebrates on a California beach to exceed 300 species. While many are rare and reclusive, forty or more might be visible to a casual observer.

Opposite: *Common dolphins travel at speeds up to twenty-five miles per hour.*
RICHARD HERRMANN
Above left: *At first glance, the sea anemone resembles a chrysanthemum, but the anemone's "petals" are actually tentacles.*
JEFF FOOTT
Above right: *An elephant seal pup nuzzles its mother in search of her rich milk.*
JACK D. SWENSON

One may find the red abalone, a favorite food of man and sea otter, or the periwinkle, a marine snail that feeds on algae film on rocks. In other areas the rocks are covered with barnacles, which catch drifting bits of plankton and food when covered with water but seal up tight at low tide when exposed to sun and air.

Included in the intertidal zone are grazing animals like limpets and snails. Deeper in the tide pools are found the elegant sea anemone, giant green anemone, red rock crab, and hermit crab, which adopts a snail shell as its home, carrying it across the sand as it travels. Predators of the tide pools include several species of sea stars that feed on snails, limpets, and other life.

In the deepest tide pools are found still other sea stars and sea urchins. The large sunflower star prowls the lower pools, sending snails, sea urchins, and abalones nearly galloping away in panic. Many interesting and diverse species of crabs, shrimps, snails, slugs, and of course,

---

Above left: Pelagia colorata *is one of the marine invertebrates that awaits the explorer beneath the ocean's surface.*
RICHARD HERRMANN
Above right: *Besides starfish, the glaucous-* *winged gull feeds on the young of ducks and other coastal birds.*
MIKE DANZENBAKER
Opposite: *A beautiful Spanish shawl floats off the California Coast.*
JEFF FOOTT

---

fish provide opportunities for natural history studies. The variety of life and the extraordinary adaptations needed to survive all help make California's coastal edge productive and unforgettable.

After the luxurious diversity under the tides, life on the beach seems simple and transitory. Few wild species live continually on the sand, finding it a desert-like environment between the fertile tide pools and productive salt marshes. The rare least tern and the snowy plover are two birds that prefer a sandy beach for nesting. Both have been seriously affected by human activity.

Gulls and migrant shorebirds use the beach for foraging on a regular basis. One of the most

common is the sanderling, a small sandpiper which travels in flocks, moving in and out with the tide to feed on small invertebrates under the sand. In the dunes behind the beaches are found the white-crowned sparrow and shy grasshopper sparrow. Also in the dunes and visiting the beach to feed are raccoons, coyotes, and gray foxes. In the air above the dunes the northern harrier looks for the little brush rabbit or perhaps a young black-tailed jackrabbit.

Farther from the beach, one may find remnants of the coastal salt marsh environment. Much more common on the Atlantic and Gulf coasts because of the shallow ocean floor, such environments, which must have protection from the pounding surf, are rare in California.

Most are a part of the San Francisco Bay complex. Another major salt marsh is found in Humboldt Bay. Some estimates place the total acreage of salt marshes in the state at only 56,000 acres, about one-twentieth of 1 percent of the state's land area.

Despite their drab and bleak appearance, salt marshes are among the world's most produc-

Above: *Pacific white-sided dolphins often gather in schools of several hundred. On a peaceful day, a feeding school's deep inhalations resonate across the still water.*
MARK J. RAUZON

Opposite: *On the California Coast, tidepools bring many creatures close to the surface, including this purple shore crab, also found in the mud of salt marshes.*
JEFF FOOTT

tive ecosystems. They serve as nursery grounds for many animal species that move out of the marshes with the tide into the sea. Few bird species reside in the tide marshes; of the five that do, four are regarded as endangered. The small salt marsh harvest mouse, another marsh resident, is on both state and federal endangered species lists.

Although there are few permanent residents, the marshes attract many different visitors and millions of migrating waterfowl, wading birds, and other birdlife, each cycling in and out of the marsh depending on the tidal pulse. While birdlife is abundant, few mammals are found in the marshes except for raccoons and an occasional striped skunk.

Much of the critical marshland has been lost in Southern California, and after years of decline in the San Francisco Bay, the pattern of development has begun to change. At one time the marshes were constantly being filled for airports, garbage dumps, warehouses, highways, and housing developments. Today every wetland development is challenged, and marsh restoration plans and programs are required. Restoration of historic marshlands will be increasingly the focus of wildlife conservation. Fortunately, where these efforts have been attempted, the natural productivity of the environment helps speed restoration and rehabilitation. Nature's ability to heal itself, given the opportunity, is encouraging and refreshing, and especially critical for the salt marsh. ■

The California least tern

Officially listed as endangered, the California least tern *(Sterna albifrons browni)* is on its way to recovery. One of three beach-nesting terns in the United States, the California tern arrives in the state during April. Courtship soon begins involving the male carrying a small fish in its beak and calling for a female. Later a pair will fly in formation and carry out elaborate flight patterns. Courtship and mating conclude with a ritual feeding of the female by the male.

Nests are simply scraped in the sandy beach and the egg laid on a depression in the sand. All breeding pairs nest in colonies and return to the same beach each year. The young hatch in three weeks and are soon wandering around with other chicks on the beach. Somehow the parents feed only their own young, and the chicks respond only to their parents' calls.

The terns' habit of nesting and raising their young on beaches was a major cause of their decline after World War II. As beaches were developed, vehicles and people trampled their nests. Although the birds nested successfully on parking lots, freeway cloverleafs, and airport runways, their numbers declined year after year.

Several conservation laws, including both the federal and state endangered species acts and the California Coastal Zone Act, provided for planning and protection of critical nesting habitats. Old nesting sites were closed and protected during the breeding season and papier-mâché decoys used to attract new nesting pairs. Predators like feral cats, skunks, opossum, and others were controlled to help the recovery. Starting from a low of 600 pairs, the California least tern now numbers over 1,000 pairs. Knowledge of the bird's life history is sufficient to assure its continued recovery. ■

99

Opposite: *The snowy egret can be identified by its yellow feet, black legs, and brilliant white plumage. This elegant bird once faced extinction because its plumes were fashionable.*
MIKE DANZENBAKER

Above: *A male least tern offers a tasty fish to his nesting mate. Because of efforts to protect its nesting beaches, this bird is now recovering from near extinction.*
TUPPER ANSEL BLAKE

Whale watching

The return of the great whales to the world's oceans is a landmark environmental success story. It has also spawned a new industry off the California Coast: whale watching. The Pacific Coast is the best place in the world to see the great whales, and the California Coast has more exceptional viewing areas than anywhere else.

A wide range of private charter operators are available to take whale watchers out for sightings in any major coastal city. While the tours vary in length and quality, many are available for two and a half to three hours. In Southern California in 1987 there were twenty-four companies operating one hundred ships carrying tens of thousands of whale watchers.

On the West Coast thirty of the seventy-six known species of whales, dolphins, and porpoises can be seen. Most people are attracted to the "great whales," twenty-five feet or longer in size. Ten of the twelve species are found off the western shore.

From coastal viewpoints the most common whale is the gray. They begin to appear off the coast of Northern California on their southern

migration in December, peaking in January. The northern migration starts off the southern coast in March and continues into May. Blue and humpback whales are seen offshore in deep water from July through October.

A few of the many places to view the gray whale migration are:

Vista location along Highway 101 south of Crescent City; Redwood National Park in Humboldt County; Gold Bluffs Campground off Highway 101 at Davidson Road turnoff; Luffenholtz Beach and Holuda Point, two miles south of Trinidad; Clam Beach County Park, 3.5 miles north of McKinleyville; Table Bluff County Park at the town of Beatrice; high bluffs along Highway 1 from Rockport to Inglenook; bluffs along Highway 1 near Fort Bragg; MacKerricher State Park at Laguna Point, north of Fort Bragg.

Jug Handle State Reserve, .5 mile north of Caspar; roadside viewing areas on Highway 1 near Mendocino; Russian Gulch State Park north of Mendocino; Mendocino Headlands State Park in Mendocino; Mallo Pass Creek Vista Point, 4.5 miles north of Manchester State Beach; overlooks along Highway 1 near the town of Point Arena; Collins Landing, four miles north of the Sonoma-Mendocino County line; vantage points along Highway 1 from Sonoma-Mendocino County line to Jenner.

Blufftop Trail, north of the town of Stewarts Point; Salt Point State Park, twenty miles north of the town of Jenner; Sonoma Coast state

beaches between the Russian River outlet to Bodega Head; Bodega Head at the west side of Bodega Bay; several points at Point Reyes National Seashore; several points in Golden Gate National Recreation Area.

In San Francisco, Cliff House at Lincoln Park and Geary Boulevard; Gray Whale Cove State Beach, 1.5 miles north of Montara; San Gregorio, Pomponio, and Pescadero state beaches in San Gregorio; Lighthouse Field State Beach in Santa Cruz; Año Nuevo State Reserve on Highway 1; lookout points along twelve-mile drive in Carmel and Point Lobos State Reserve; many lookout points along Highway 1 from Monterey to San Simeon; Montana De Oro State Park and Cambria Pines Beach in San Luis Obispo County; Gaviota State Park and Refugio State Beach near Point Conception.

Carpinteria State Beach, three miles north of Ventura County line in Carpinteria; Point Mugu Beach, south of Oxnard off Highway 1; Point Dume Whale Watch off Highway 1 in Malibu; Flat Rock Point in Palos Verdes Estates; Laguna Beach, Crescent Bay Point Park, and Heisler Park in Orange County; Solana Beach County Park north of San Diego; Torrey Pines City Park and Torrey Pines City Beach south of Del Mar; Ellen Browning Scripps Memorial Park in Point La Jolla; Cabrillo National Monument at Point Loma.

Above: *Whale watching from the Point Reyes National Seashore lighthouse is a popular activity, bringing millions of dollars into the California economy.*
JEFF FOOTT

Opposite: *The graceful tail flukes of the massive sperm whale drive this sixty-ton mammal throughout the oceans of the world and along the coast of California.*
WILLIAM ERVIN

Peaceful coexistence

If a war of races should occur between the wild beasts and Lord Man, I would be tempted to sympathize with the bears.

—John Muir

Until recently, development in California rapidly eliminated and altered natural environments without any understanding of the consequences, nor any discussion. As a result, 220 wildlife species, 600 types of plants, and many entire natural communities are near extinction. But environmental organizations continue to grow and expand their educational roles and political clout. Environmental law builds more and more layers of protection for natural communities. Most important, developers are learning that environmental protection and restoration are normal costs of doing business, not some passing fad.

Once thought to be a merely aesthetic concern, biological diversity is becoming more appreciated as a source of flood and fire protection, pest management, and a means of reducing air and water pollution. An expanding array of foods and medicines also derive from those plants and animals that thrive in a biologically diverse environment.

The many species either now listed or threatened with elimination make the task of assuring biological diversity dismaying. However, conservation organizations have repeatedly demonstrated that success is possible. Research may be needed. Time and money are required. Political will is the scarce ingredient.

California, compared with other states, has well-developed laws designed to protect many aspects of its resources. These include the California Endangered Species Act, the Wildlife Conservation Law, and the California Environmental Quality Act. Other laws protecting biological diversity include the Wetlands Preservation Act, the Native Species Conservation and Enhancement Act, the state's Wild and Scenic Rivers Act, and the California Wilderness Act. Partial protection of native endangered plants is offered in the Native Plant Protection Act.

California's federal lands are protected under several important laws, including the Wilderness Act, the Wild and Scenic Rivers Act, the Federal Land Policy and Management Act, and the National Forest Management Act. Several other federal laws protect water quality, regulate dredging and filling of the tidelands, and provide for regulation and management of pesticides, herbicides, and other chemicals.

In keeping with California's leadership tradition, conservationists developed a 1988 ballot initiative, Proposition 70, the California Wildlife, Coastal, and Parks Initiative. It has been called the boldest and most far-reaching wildlife initiative ever written and offered to voters. Designed to raise $776 million through the sale of general obligation bonds for the purpose of purchasing riparian, park, and wildlife habitat, it passed by a two-to-one margin in the June 1988 election. Some eighty sites will be acquired throughout the state, many of them of critical importance to endangered species.

Also in 1988, after years of negotiation over a class action suit filed against one of the state's major banks, California State Controller Gray Davis concluded the case by accepting several thousand acres of land previously owned by the bank as a part of the settlement. The land was dedicated to habitat protection.

Most people believe the conservation of biological diversity cannot rely solely on sanctions and criminal law. The best approach, in the long run, is education. In 1980, a model wildlife education project was established cooperatively among the fish and game departments of several western states, national wildlife conservation

Opposite: *The extraordinary bird life at Mono Lake—including these phalaropes—depends directly on adequate and continued water supplies.*
GALEN ROWELL

Right: *Once endangered by pesticides and hunters, the bald eagle is now expanding its population in California and elsewhere.*
LEWIS KEMPER

organizations such as Defenders of Wildlife, and the Western Regional Environmental Education Council. Project WILD, Wildlife in Learning Design, was the result. Project WILD encourages young people to make intelligent judgments and informed choices about conservation and land-use issues.

In the future habitat acquisition must be hastened. At the same time, damaged environments must be restored. Stronger laws for endangered species and an accelerated process of listing and protection are needed. Conservation through market pricing of agricultural water would be a major step toward assuring instream flows on many rivers. Much can be done to encourage conservation efforts on private land through tax and other incentive programs. Land developments affecting critical environments require continued research and effective management.

Given a chance nature will respond.

Over a hundred years ago, while rambling in the Sierras, John Muir posed some of the same questions we face today regarding California's environmental future:

Will human destructions like those of Nature—fire and flood and avalanche—work out a higher good, a finer beauty? Will a better civilization come in accord with obvious nature . . . ? And what then is coming? What is the human part of the mountains' destiny? ■

The peregrine falcon—a conservation success story

The world's fastest and most inspiring aerial predator, the peregrine falcon *(Falco peregrinus)* has been admired for hundreds of years. Because of its popularity and awesome hunting style, the bird's population crash in the 1950s was watched with increasing alarm. Research established the link between DDT and thin eggshells that was leading to near total loss of the young. Nationally as well as in California, a campaign was launched to ban the pesticide. With the massive publicity generated by Rachel Carson's *Silent Spring*, this ban was accomplished.

Immediately after the passage of the En-dangered Species Act, the peregrine was listed as endangered. At several locations around the country, research led to breeding programs, captive rearing of the young, and hacking, or releasing young adults into the wild. In busy urban areas the common pigeon, grown soft from city life, was docile prey for the dynamic falcon, and soon falcons were nesting outside the windows of busy corporate offices high above the urban traffic.

In the 1940s California hosted at least a hundred breeding pairs of peregrine falcons. By the early 1970s there were less than ten pairs statewide. Once biologists went to work, however, some of these remaining pairs were exceptionally prolific. One female nesting on Morro Rock between 1976 and 1986 laid a total of fifty-four eggs and contributed twenty young to California skies.

By 1986 the peregrine's flight to recovery was definitely underway. At least forty-three pairs were in the wild that year, and they raised fifty-three young. (In contrast, for several years in the 1950s, not one young was successfully raised.) In addition, eighty-two birds reared in captivity were released into the wilds. ∎

Opposite: *California's black bears continue to survive in the state's parks and remote areas. Illegal hunting of the bear is the focus of enforcement efforts.*
D. CAVAGNARO

Above: *Able to dive at speeds approaching 200 miles per hour, the peregrine falcon is the world's fastest bird. It is no longer on the brink of extinction.*
TUPPER ANSEL BLAKE

Where to watch wildlife

California's public lands, national forests, wildlife refuges, and state and federal parks afford many opportunities for viewing wildlife. However, wildlife can also be observed from busy highways, bridges spanning the San Francisco Bay, or in a quiet backyard. The key to locating wildlife is finding suitable habitat and having the proper timing.

The ecological principle known as the "edge effect" will help you recognize wildlife habitat. Many animals live on the "edge" of dense woods, meadows, marshes, or other environments, resting and taking shelter in the forest but venturing into open areas for food. At these edges you will find trails, tracks, and droppings to help identify both the type of animal and its habits. Guidebooks to birds, wildlife, tracks, and other aspects of nature will quickly improve your observation skills. Use binoculars or a spotting scope with tripod for optimum viewing without disturbing the animals. Some telescopes can be adapted to your camera to provide a photographic record.

The most productive times to view wildlife are early in the morning and late in the evening. Stealth and patience are also important. In many areas seasonal timing is essential. For example, alpine environments are largely empty during the winter months but active and productive during the summer. Spring finds wetlands anywhere teeming with life. Summer in the desert can give the impression the region is void of life, but the experienced viewer finds a well-worn path, a spring or seep of water, and waits. When the sun begins to drop from sight,

the desert comes alive with deer, coyote, and other animals trekking in from their daytime shelter for water.

This guide will help you locate some of the most productive areas for viewing wildlife on public lands. Maps and additional information are available from the following offices:

Department of Fish and Game
1416 Ninth Street
Sacramento, CA 95814
(916) 445-3531
The Fish and Game Department has responsibility for protection and management of fish and wildlife in the state.

Department of Parks and Recreation
1416 Ninth Street
P.O. Box 942896
Sacramento, CA 94296-0001
(916) 445-6477
California has over 300 state parks, one of the largest systems in the nation.

East Bay Regional Park District
11500 Skyline Blvd.
Oakland, CA 94619
(415) 531-9300
Rivaling some state park systems, the East Bay Regional Park District has locations in Contra Costa and Alameda counties.

Opposite: *Freshwater marshes and riparian forests along the Sacramento River are among the state's most endangered habitats. Fortunately, they can be salvaged and conserved, and several organizations are working to protect this vital region.*
TUPPER ANSEL BLAKE

National wildlife refuges

Colusa NWR
c/o Sacramento NWR
Route 1
Box 311
Willows, CA 95988
(916) 934-2801
This 4,000-acre marsh and cropland area is located one-half mile west of Colusa on Highway 20.

Delevan NWR
c/o Sacramento NWR
Route 1
Box 311
Willows, CA 95988
(916) 934-2801
Located four miles west of Maxwell on Maxwell Road, Delevan includes 5,600 acres of marsh and cropland.

Farallon Islands NWR
c/o San Fransisco Bay NWR
P. O. Box 524
Newark, CA 94560-0524
(415) 792-0222
These islands are 30 miles west of San Francisco in the Pacific Ocean. Refuge land is not accessible to the public, but wildlife can be viewed from private boats and commercial tours. The 140 acres of islands are the largest seabird rookery south of Alaska, hosting 200,000 birds each summer. California and Steller sea lions, elephant seals, and harbor seals all breed and pup here.

Kern NWR
Box 219
Delano, CA 93216
(805) 725-2767
Located 19 miles west of Delano on Garces Avenue

or east of I-5 on Highway 46, these 10,600 acres of valley grassland and marsh are best for viewing September through May, but the season varies from year to year because of the water supply. It is a wintering area for migratory waterfowl, shorebirds, and marsh dwellers when water is available. It also provides habitat for the endangered San Joaquin kit fox and blunt-nosed leopard lizard. Striped and spotted skunks, desert cottontail, and black-tailed jackrabbit are common.

Kesterson NWR
c/o San Luis NWR
P.O. Box 2176
Los Banos, CA 93635
(209) 826-3508

This refuge is 18 miles north of the headquarters and 4 miles east of Gustine on Highway 140. Almost 6,000 acres of seasonal marsh are used by large wintering groups of mallards, gadwell, and geese. Spring and fall bring phalaropes, sandpipers, and curlews. Although the refuge has received national attention over selenium contamination, it remains an important wildlife area.

Klamath Basin NWR
Route 1
Box 74
Tulelake, CA 96134
(916) 677-2231

Lower Klamath, located 24 miles south of Klamath Falls, Oregon, has 21,400 acres of water and marshland. Over one million waterfowl are found in this refuge during the fall migration. Also found are up to 500 bald eagles in the winter, as well as approximately 250,000 snow geese. There are antelope, marmots, and mule deer any time of the year.

Merced NWR
c/o San Luis NWR
P.O. Box 2176
Los Banos, CA 93635
(209) 826-3508

This refuge is 14 miles southwest of Merced. Within the 2,560 acres of marsh are found wintering ducks and geese. The spring and fall seasons bring sandpipers, curlews, and phalaropes. Summer finds avocets, bitterns, stilts, herons, and egrets.

Modoc NWR
Box 1610
Alturas, CA 96101
(503) 947-3315

Located 3.5 miles southeast of Alturas, this area holds 6,280 acres of ponds and marsh. Large concentrations of waterfowl are found in the spring and fall. There is nesting habitat for sandhill cranes, and white pelicans are seen during the summer. Mule deer and pronghorn antelope are the major large wildlife species.

Sacramento NWR
Route 1
Box 311
Willows, CA 95988
(916) 934-2801

The refuge is 6 miles south of Willows on old Highway 99W. 10,800 acres of marsh and cropland serve as a winter refuge for migratory waterfowl such as the endangered Aleutian Canada goose and the rare tule white-fronted goose. Red fox, skunk, muskrat, and ringtail are residents as well.

Salinas River Wildlife Management Area
c/o San Fransisco Bay NWR
P. O. Box 524
Newark, CA 94560-0524
(415) 792-0222

Located 11 miles northeast of Monterey via the Del Monte Road exit from Highway 1, these 500 acres of salt marsh, beach, and lagoon hold the endangered California clapper rail and brown pelican. In addition, many common shorebirds and waterfowl are regular inhabitants.

Salton Sea NWR
906 W. Sinclair Road
Calipatria, CA 92233
(619) 348-5278

At the south end of the Salton Sea off I-8 or State Route 111, these 35,000 acres of salt marsh and open water are 228 feet below sea level and attract tropical marine birds during the summer. However, the most numerous waterfowl are found during December and January.

San Francisco Bay NWR
P. O. Box 524
Newark, CA 94560-0524
(415) 792-0222

Refuge headquarters is east of Dumbarton Bridge Toll Plaza on Highway 84. There are 23,000 acres of salt marshes, ponds, and estuaries. Harbor seals with their pups can be seen, and five endangered species: California least tern, California clapper rail, salt marsh harvest mouse, brown pelican, and peregrine falcon.

San Luis NWR
P. O. Box 2176
Los Banos, CA 93635
(209) 826-3508

Located near Los Banos, 10 miles to the northwest on County Road J-14, this 7,300-acre refuge of water, marsh, and cropland hosts large wintering populations of pintails, teal, shovelers, and other waterfowl. On land, the endangered San Joaquin kit fox and tule elk share the area with avocets, herons, and egrets.

San Pablo Bay NWR
c/o San Fransisco NWR
P. O. Box 524
Newark, CA 94560-0524
(415) 792-0222

Found 12 miles west of Vallejo and 7 miles east of Novato off Highway 37, this refuge includes 12,000 acres of salt marsh and tidal flats which host the endangered California clapper rail and the salt marsh harvest mouse. Coyotes, bobcats, and many thousands of shore and marsh birds share this area with rafts of as many as 5,000 canvasbacks during the winter.

Opposite: *Because it requires a clean and wild coast to survive, the clever sea otter remains the most sensitive measure of the health of the California coastline.*

TOM AND PAT LEESON

Sutter NWR
c/o Sacramento NWR
Route 1
Box 311
Willows, CA 95988
(916) 934-2801

Located two miles south of Sutter, this refuge holds 2,600 acres of marshland and cropland.

National forests

Angeles National Forest
701 N. Santa Anita Ave.
Arcadia, CA 91006,
(818) 574-1613

693,454 acres. This national forest contains rugged mountains of fir and pine varying to chaparral at the lowest levels. Bighorn sheep, mountain lion, black bear, coyote, and bobcat are all found.

Cleveland National Forest
880 Front Street
San Diego, CA 92188
(619) 557-5050

420,000 acres. Rugged mountain forests lead to chaparral on the lower slopes. Major wildlife seen are bald eagle, mountain lion, bobcat, ringtail, and bighorn sheep.

Eldorado National Forest
100 Forni Road
Placerville, CA 95667
(916) 622-5061

671,000 acres. The habitat here ranges from the Sierra Nevada foothills to alpine areas where pine and fir forest dominate. Major wildlife includes black bear, mule deer, mountain lion, bobcat, and coyote.

Inyo National Forest
873 North Main St.
Bishop CA 93514
(619) 873-5841

1,800,000 acres. At high elevations, this forest features the largest groves of bristlecone pines in the world, some of which are over 4,000 years old. Extremely rugged mountains with pine and fir forests and Great Basin sagebrush provide habitat for California

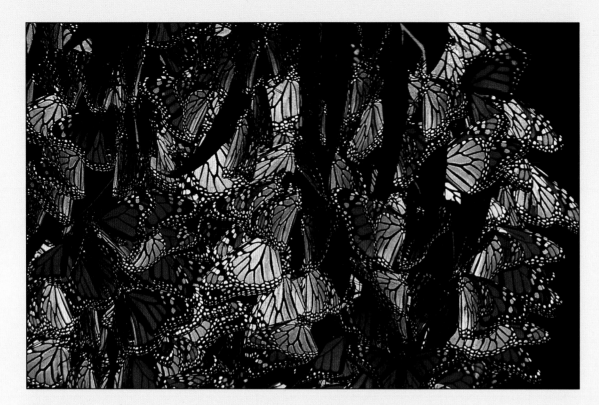

110

bighorn sheep, tule elk, Sierra red fox, and golden trout.

Klamath National Forest
1312 Fairlane Road
Yreka, CA 96097
(916) 842-6131

1,680,000 acres. Dense and rugged rainforest lie in the western sections of this forest. The eastern area is dominated by fir and pine forests among volcanic mountains and features such major wildlife as bald eagle, black bear, mountain lion, bobcat, and the rare Siskiyou mountain salamander.

Lassen National Forest
55 S. Sacramento St.
Susanville, CA 96130
(916) 257-2151

1,060,000 acres. The volcanic features of this area are largely covered by fir and pine forests occupied by black bear, osprey, mule deer, mountain lion, and

the threatened bald eagle.

Los Padres National Forest
6144 Calle Real
Goleta, CA 93117
(805) 683-6711

1,752,000 acres. Rugged pine- and fir-covered mountains and rare bristlecone fir are found on the higher peaks. Lower elevations include redwoods and chaparral habitats. Major wildlife includes bald eagle, peregrine falcon, San Joaquin kit fox, and mountain lion.

Mendocino National Forest
420 East Laurel St.
Willows, CA 95988
(916) 934-3316

882,000 acres. The higher elevations consist of pine and fir forests. The eastern portion is rugged, with complex plant communities. Major wildlife includes bald eagle, bear, bobcat, and mountain lion.

Modoc National Forest
441 N. Main St.
Alturas, CA 96101
(916) 233-5811

1,654,000 acres. This region includes alpine lakes, grassy meadows, and pine and fir forest. Juniper forests dominate eastern regions in the Great Basin area. The major wildlife are black bear, golden eagle, mountain lion, and mule deer.

Plumas National Forest
159 Lawrence St.
Box 11500
Quincy, CA 95971
(916) 283-2050

1,164,000 acres. The pine and fir forests in this rugged volcanic setting include many impressive mountain meadows and wildlife such as black bear, osprey, bald eagle, coyote, and mule deer.

San Bernardino National Forest
1824 Commercenter Circle
San Bernardino, CA 92408
(714) 383-5588

810,000 acres. With pine and fir at higher elevations, these rugged mountains are dominated by chaparral. The major wildlife are bighorn sheep, golden and bald eagle, acorn woodpecker, great horned owl, and mountain lion.

Sequoia National Forest
900 West Grand Ave.
Porterville, CA 93257
(209) 784-1500

1,125,000 acres. This national forest includes the largest sequoia in the world on the lower western slopes and dwarf fir, with rugged mountains and alpine lakes at higher elevations. You can see bald eagle, peregrine falcon, golden trout, blunt-nosed leopard lizard, and bighorn sheep.

Shasta-Trinity National Forest
2400 Washington Ave.
Redding, CA 96001
(916) 246-5222

2,154,000 acres. Dense forests, mountain meadows, and deep canyons surround 14,000-foot Mt. Shasta. The golden eagle, black bear, mountain lion, bobcat, and mule deer live here.

Sierra National Forest
1130 O Street
Room 3017
Fresno, CA 93721
(209) 487-5155

1,300,000 acres. These national lands include large groves of sequoia at lower levels as well as ponderosa pine. Lodgepole pine, red fir, and alpine species are found at higher levels on rugged mountains and clear, cold lakes. In these settings you can see black bear, wolverine, mule deer, marten, and fisher.

Six Rivers National Forest
507 F Street
Eureka, CA 95501
(707) 442-1781

980,000 acres. Dense redwood and rainforest are located at lower elevations. Cedar, alder, pine, and fir stands mix with oaks and willows. This is a complex forest system with black bear, mountain lion, Roosevelt elk, mountain beaver, and coyote.

Stanislaus National Forest
19777 Greenley Road
Sonora, CA 95370
(209) 532-3671

899,000 acres. Dense pine and fir forests vary with open and rugged alpine lakes and meadows. Black bear, mountain lion, coyote, and mule deer can all be seen.

Tahoe National Forest
Highway 49
Nevada City, CA 95959
(916) 265-4531

813,000 acres. Fir, lodgepole pine, and other alpine species at higher elevations surround rugged basins. Lower down the slopes are stands of mixed conifers and hardwoods. The foothills are drier, with oak and grassland. In this varied landscape the wildlife includes bald and golden eagle, peregrine falcon, Lahonton cutthroat trout, black bear, mountain lion, and wolverine.

National parks

Channel Islands National Park
1901 Spinnaker Drive
Ventura, CA 93001
(805) 644-8157

249,000 acres. A total of 8 islands with rocky beaches is located 10 to 20 miles off the California Coast. Major wildlife includes fur seal, sea lion, elephant seal, sea otter, island fox, blue whale, humpback whale, and many seabirds.

Lassen Volcanic National Park
Mineral, CA 96063
(916) 595-4444

106,000 acres. Exceptional mountain meadows are surrounded by fir and pine forest and rugged volcanic peaks. Major wildlife includes mule deer, black bear, marmot, chickaree, and fox squirrel.

Point Reyes National Seashore
Point Reyes, CA 94956
(415) 663-8522

64,500 acres. Long, open beaches, sea cliffs, and lagoons are near forested ridges and offshore rocks. Major wildlife species are fallow deer, tule elk, sea lion, mountain lion, bobcat, and many seabirds.

Redwood National Park
1111 Second St.
Crescent City, CA 95531
(707) 464-6101

110,000 acres. Dense and wet redwood forest located in the coastal fog belt includes areas that have been logged. There is a coastal zone as well. Roosevelt elk, black bear, mountain lion, mule deer, seal, and sea lion are all present.

Sequoia and Kings Canyon national parks
Three Rivers, CA 93271
(209) 565-3341

864,000 acres. Giant sequoia forest and mixed conifer forest are found on lower slopes with higher elevations showing alpine lakes, meadows, and rugged mountain views. Major wildlife includes black bear, mule deer, pine marten, fisher, wolverine, and bighorn sheep.

Opposite: *Unlike most of their kind, monarch butterflies gather in large numbers and migrate to wintering areas on the California Coast. The preservation of the monarch's native food supply is essential.*
RON SANFORD

Yosemite National Park
CA 95389
(209) 372-4461

761,000 acres. Alpine lakes and meadows with rugged Sierra mountains vary with lower-elevation coniferous forest including great sequoia. Major wildlife forms are black bear, mule deer, bighorn sheep, pine marten, wolverine, and bald eagle.

Bureau of Land Management

Bakersfield District
800 Truxton Ave.
Room 302
Bakersfield, CA 93301
(805) 861-4191

1,700,000 acres. Scattered Central Valley and foothill land is mixed with private ranches. Mule deer, kit fox, bobcat, and coyote can be found.

California Desert District
1695 Spruce St.
Riverside, CA 92507
(714) 351-6394

12,100,000 acres. This district is largely Mojave Desert and rugged desert mountains. A diverse and impressive region, it is proposed for national park and wilderness status. Major wildlife includes mule deer, desert bighorn, and wild burros.

Susanville District
705 Hall Street
Susanville, CA 96130
(916) 257-5381

1,370,000 acres. Largely Great Basin valleys and plateaus, this area has sagebrush flats and pinyon forests with major wildlife such as pronghorns, wild horses, mule deer, and coyotes.

Ukiah District
555 Leslie Street
P.O. Box 940
Ukiah, CA 95482
(707) 462-3873

640,000 acres. Scattered tracts of foothill and coastal range parcels are mixed with private land. Major wildlife includes mule deer, black bear, and coyote. ■

Also available in the California Geographic Series ...

California Deserts, Book Three
by Jerry Schad

Explore the vast, enigmatic Mojave and Colorado deserts of Southern California through gorgeous color photographs taken by acclaimed outdoor photographers and a fascinating text. Featuring the East Mojave National Scenic Area and other parts of the California Desert Conservation Area, Joshua Tree National Monument, Death Valley National Monument, and Anza-Borrego Desert State Park, *California Deserts* offers an unforgettable excursion through the hottest, driest, lowest, and loveliest places in North America.

104 pp., 11" x 8½", 112 color photos, $14.95 softcover, $19.95 hardcover.

California State Parks, Book Two
by Kim Heacox

Take a journey of discovery through California's historical parks, recreation areas, wildernesses, scenic reserves, and underwater parks—over 235 in all—with *California State Parks*. Let this lively, informative book with its breathtaking color photos from the country's finest photographers immerse you in California's abundant natural beauty and colorful history. Whether you're interested in scenery, science, recreation, or history, you'll find it in *California State Parks*. An eighteen-page guide highlights the attractions and facilities available in each park to make planning a visit—or a vacation—easy.

128 pp., 11" x 8½", 120 color photos, $14.95 softcover, $19.95 hardcover.

California Mountain Ranges, Book One by Russell B. Hill

California Mountain Ranges explores the wonders, the history, and the majesty of the state's mountains through lavish photography from America's best photographers and a crisp, intriguing text. Discover plants that survive where nothing else can, wildlife that exists nowhere else, and men and women who attempted what no one thought possible. First in the California Geographic Series, this book portrays a land of fantastic cliffs, eerie hollows, desolate moonscapes, and gentle hills, providing a unique insight into some of the Golden State's most spectacular geographic features.

120 pp. 11" x 8½", 120 color photos, $14.95 softcover, $19.95 hardcover.

California Geographic Series poster

Photographer David Muench captures the mystery of redwoods shrouded in fog in this beautiful photo from *California Mountain Ranges*. 20" x 28", 12-point paper, $5.00.

To order...

California Wildlife, California Deserts, California State Parks, California Mountain Ranges, and the California Geographic Series poster: Call toll-free 1-800-582-BOOK to order with Visa or Mastercard. Or send a check or money order and include $1.50 postage and handling for each book to Falcon Press, P.O. Box 1718, Helena, MT 59624.

Our Guarantee:

If you are not satisfied with any book, calendar, or poster obtained from Falcon Press, simply return your purchase for a full refund.